# Critters
of **Florida**

## Pocket Guide to Animals in Your State

# ALEX TROUTMAN

produced in cooperation with
**Wildlife Forever**

# About Wildlife Forever

Wildlife Forever works to conserve America's outdoor heritage through conservation education, preservation of habitat, and scientific management of fish and wildlife. Wildlife Forever is a 501c3 nonprofit organization dedicated to restoring habitat and teaching the next generation about conservation. Become a member and learn more about innovative programs like the Art of Conservation®, The Fish and Songbird Art Contests®, Clean Drain Dry Initiative™, and Prairie City USA®. For more information, visit wildlifeforever.org.

*Thank you to Ann McCarthy, the original creator of the Critters series, for her dedication to wildlife conservation and to environmental education. Ann dedicates her work to her daughters, Megan and Katharine Anderson.*

Front cover photos by **Kit Leong/shutterstock.com:** panther, **Phillippe Clement/shutterstock.com:** alligator, **mattthi/shutterstock.com:** roseate spoonbill; Back cover photo by **Henry Collins Photography/Shutterstock.com:** belted kingfisher

Edited by Brett Ortler and Jenna Barron
Cover and book design by Jonathan Norberg
Proofreader: Emily Beaumont

10 9 8 7 6 5 4 3 2 1

**Critters of Florida**
First Edition 2000, Second Edition 2023

Published by Adventure Publications, an imprint of AdventureKEEN
310 Garfield Street South, Cambridge, Minnesota 55008
(800) 678-7006
www.adventurepublications.net
All rights reserved
Printed in China
LCCN 2023032578 (print); 2023032579 (ebook)
ISBN 978-1-64755-409-5 (pbk.); 978-1-64755-410-1 (ebook)

# Acknowledgments

I want to thank everyone who believed in and supported me over the years—a host of friends, family, and teachers. I want to especially thank my mom and my siblings Van, Bre, and TJ.

# Dedication

I dedicate this book to my brother Van:
May you continue to enjoy the birds and wildlife in heaven.

This book is for all the kids who have a passion for nature and the outdoors, especially ones who identify as Black, Brown, Indigenous, and People of Color. May this be an encouragement to never give up, and if you have a dream and passion for something, pursue it relentlessly. I also hope to set an example that you can be successful as your full, authentic self!

Lastly, I dedicate this book to all those with ADHD and dyslexia, as well as all other members of the neurodivergent community. While our quirks make things more challenging, our goals are not impossible to reach; sometimes it takes a little more time and help, but we, too, can succeed!

# Contents

## Mammals

## Birds

## Reptiles and Amphibians

# Introduction

My passion for nature started when I was young. I was always amazed by the sunlit fiery glow of the red-tailed hawks as they soared overhead when I went fishing with my family. The red-tailed hawk was my spark bird—the bird that captures your attention and gets you into birding. Through my many encounters with red-tailed hawks, and other species like garter snakes and coyotes, I found a passion for nature and the environment. Stumbling across conservationists like Steve Irwin, Jeff Corwin, and Jack Hanna introduced me to the field of Wildlife Biology as a career and gave birth to a dream that I was able to accomplish and live out: serving as a Fish and Wildlife Biologist for governmental agencies, as well as in the private sector.

My childhood dream was driven by a desire to learn more about the different types of ecosystems and the animals that call our wild places home. Books and field guides like this one whet my thirst for knowledge. Even before I could fully understand the words on the pages, I was drawn to books and flashcards that had animals on them. I could soon identify every animal I was shown and tell a fact about it. I hope that this edition of *Critters of Florida* can be the fuel that sustains your passion for not only learning about wildlife, but also for caring for the environment and making sure that all are welcome in the outdoors. For others, may this book be the spark that ignites a flame for wildlife preservation and environmental stewardship. I hope that this book inspires children from lower socioeconomic and minority backgrounds to pursue their dreams to the fullest and be unapologetically themselves.

By profession, I'm a Fish and Wildlife Biologist, and I'm a nature enthusiast through and through. My love for nature includes making sure that everyone has an equal opportunity to enjoy the outdoors in their own way. So, as you use this book, I encourage you to be intentional in inviting others to appreciate nature with you. Enjoy your discoveries and stay curious!

*–Alex Troutman*

# Florida: The Sunshine State

Florida is known for its beautiful beaches, tropical weather, and numerous theme parks. The first people who called Florida home arrived more than 14,000 years ago. Many different Indigenous groups have called, or still call, Florida home. The list includes the Seminole, the Miccosukee, the Creek, the Apalachee, the Timucua, and many others.

Florida is a peninsula, which means it's a piece of land almost entirely surrounded by water but still connected to the mainland. It has the Atlantic Ocean on its east coast, the Gulf of Mexico on its west coast, and the Straits of Florida to the south. There are many different landforms that make up Florida: The northern part of the state is hilly, with caves and sinkholes in the Marianna Lowlands in the northwest. The southern part of the state is home to Everglades National Park, which covers 1.5 million acres of wetlands and mangrove forests and is home to American alligators, Florida panthers, and many bird species.

Florida's coasts have sandy beaches, and farther south, one finds the Florida Keys, an amazing group of tropical islands where there are colorful coral reefs.

These environments are home to many animals, including 100-plus species of mammals, 530-some species of birds, and more than 140 species of reptiles and amphibians, not to mention fish, countless insects and spiders, mushrooms, plants, and more. This is your guide to the animals, birds, reptiles, and amphibians that call Florida home.

Some of Florida's most iconic plants, animals, and other natural resources are now officially recognized as state symbols. Get to know them below and see if you can spot them all! You'll probably encounter the state nickname and motto, so I've included them here too.

**State Bird:**
Northern Mockingbird

**State Shell:**
Horse Conch

**State Tree:**
Sabal Palm

**State Flower:**
Orange Blossom

**State Fish:**
Sailfish (saltwater)

**State Fish:**
Largemouth Bass (freshwater)

**State Reptile:**
American Alligator

**State Animal:**
Florida Panther

**State Nickname:**
The Sunshine State

**State Butterfly:**
Zebra Longwing

**State Motto:**
"In God We Trust"

# How to Use This Guide

This book is your introduction to some of the wonderful critters found in Florida; it includes 22 mammals, 29 birds, and 16 reptiles and amphibians. It includes some animals you probably already know, such as deer and bald eagles, but others you may not know about, such as eastern indigo snakes or anhingas. I've selected the species in this book because they are widespread (northern cardinal, page 82), abundant (white-tailed deer, page 54), or well-known, but best observed from a safe distance (American alligator, page 110).

The book is organized by types of animals: mammals, birds, and reptiles and amphibians. Within each section, the animals are in alphabetical order. If you'd like to look for a critter quickly, turn to the checklist (page 140), which you can also use to keep track of how many animals you've seen! For each species, you'll see a photo of the animal, along with neat facts and information on the animal's habitat, diet, its predators, how it raises its young, and more.

## Safety Note

Nature can be unpredictable, so don't go outdoors alone, and always tell an adult when you're going outside. All wild animals should be treated with respect. If you see one—big or small—don't get close to it or attempt to touch or feed it. Instead, keep your distance and enjoy spotting it. If you can, snap some pictures with a camera or make a quick drawing using a sketchbook. If the animal is getting too close, is acting strangely, or seems sick or injured, tell an adult right away, as it might have rabies, a disease that can affect mammals. The good news is there's a rabies vaccine, so it's important to visit a doctor right away if you get bit or scratched by a wild animal.

# Notes About Icons

Each species page includes basic information about an animal, from what it eats to how it survives the winter. The book also includes information that's neat to know; in the mammals section, each page includes a simple track illustration of the animal, with approximate track size included. And along the bottom, there is an example track pattern for the mammal, with the exception for those that primarily glide or fly (flying squirrels and bats).

On the left-hand page for each mammal, a rough-size illustration is included that shows how big the animal is when compared to a basketball.

Also on the left-hand page, there are icons that tell you when each animal is most active: nocturnal (at night), diurnal (during the day), or crepuscular (at dawn/dusk), so you know when to look. If an animal has a "zzz" icon, it hibernates during the winter. Some animals hibernate every winter, and their internal processes (breathing and heartbeat) slow down almost entirely. Other animals only partially hibernate, but this still helps them save energy and survive through the coldest part of the year.

nocturnal
(active at night)

diurnal
(active during day)

crepuscular
(most active at dawn and dusk)

hibernates/deep sleeper
(dormant during winter)

ground nest

cup nest

platform nest

cavity nest

migrates

On the left-hand side of each bird page, the nest for the species is shown, along with information on whether or not the bird migrates; on the right-hand side, there's information on where it goes.

## Did you know?

Beavers are rodents! Yes, these flat-tailed mammals are rodents, like rats and squirrels. In fact, they are the largest native rodents in North America. Just like other rodents, beavers have large incisors, which they use to chew through trees to build dams and dens. Beavers are the original wetland engineers. By damming rivers and streams, beavers create ponds and wetlands.

Size Comparison    Most Active    Track Size

# American Beaver

*Castor canadensis*

**Size:** Body is 25–30 inches long; tail is 9–13 inches long; weighs 30–70 pounds

**Habitat:** Wooded wetland areas near ponds, streams, and lakes

**Range:** Beavers can be found throughout northern Florida and the Panhandle, as well as much of the rest of the US.

**Food:** Leaves, twigs, and stems; they also feed on fruits and aquatic plant roots. Throughout the year they gather and store tree cuttings, which they eat in winter.

**Den:** A beaver's home is called a lodge. It consists of a pile of branches that is splattered with mud and vegetation. Lodges are constructed on the banks of lakes and streams and have exits and entrances that are underwater.

**Young:** Young beavers (kits) are born in late April through May and June in litters of 3–4. After two years they are considered mature and will be forced out of the den.

**Predators:** Bobcats, cougars, bears, wolves, and coyotes. Human trappers are major predators too.

**Tracks:** A beaver's front foot looks a lot like your hand; it has five fingers. The hind (back) foot is long, with five separate toes that have webbing or extra skin between them.

Beavers range from dark brown to reddish brown. They have a stocky body with hind legs that are longer than the front legs. The beaver's body is covered in dense fur, but its tail is naked and has special blood vessels that help it cool or warm its body.

**Did you know?**
Female bears weigh between 90 and 300 pounds and are smaller than the average adult human male in the US. But don't let their small size fool you; with a bite force around 800 pounds per square inch (PSI) and swiping force of over 400 pounds, these bears are not to be taken lightly.

| Size Comparison | Most Active | Track Size | Hibernates |
|:---:|:---:|:---:|:---:|
|  |  |  | |

6–7"

# Black Bear

*Ursus americanus*

**Size:** 5–6 feet long (nose to tail); weighs 90–600 pounds

**Habitat:** Forests, lowland areas, and swamps flatwoods

**Range:** Black bears can be found in many parts of North America from Alaska down through Canada and into Mexico. In Florida, black bears can be found in specific hotspots and the surrounding areas throughout the state.

**Food:** Berries, fish, seeded crops, small mammals, wild grapes, tree shoots, ants, bees, beavers, and even deer fawns

**Den:** Denning usually starts in December, with bears emerging in late March or April. Dens can be either dug (out of a hillside, for example) or constructed with materials such as leaves, grass, and moss.

**Young:** Two cubs are usually born at one time (a litter), often in January. Cubs are born without fur and blind, with pink skin. They weigh 8–16 ounces.

**Predators:** Humans and other bears. Sometimes, other carnivores, such as mountain lions, wolves, coyotes, or even bobcats, will prey on black bears. Cubs are especially vulnerable.

**Tracks:** Front print is usually 4–6 inches long and 3½–5 inches wide, with the hind foot being 6–7 inches long and 3½–5 inches wide. The feet have five toes.

Black bears are usually black in color, but they can be many different variations of black and brown. Some even have grayish, reddish, or blonde fur.

### Did you know?

Bobcats get their name from their short tail; a "bob" is a type of short haircut. They have the largest range of all wild cats in the United States. Bobcats can even hunt prey much larger than themselves; in fact, they can take down prey that is over four times their size, such as white-tailed deer!

Size Comparison   Most Active   Track Size

2"

# Bobcat

*Lynx rufus*

**Size:** 27–48 inches head to tail; males weigh around 30 pounds, while females weigh 24 pounds or so

**Habitat:** Dense forests, scrub areas (forests of low trees and bushes), swamps, and even some urban (city) areas

**Range:** They are widespread throughout the US. In Florida, they have been found throughout the state.

**Food:** Squirrels, birds, rabbits and snowshoe hares, and white-tailed deer fawns; occasionally even adult deer.

**Den:** Dense shrubs, caves, or even hollow trees; dens can be lined with leaves or moss.

**Young:** Bobcats usually breed in early winter through spring. Females give birth to a litter of 2–4 kittens. Bobcats become independent around 7–8 months, and they reach reproductive maturity at 1 year for females and at 2 years for males.

**Predators:** Occasionally fishers and coyotes; humans also hunt and trap bobcats for fur.

**Tracks:** Roughly 2 inches wide; both front and back paws have four toe pads and a carpal pad (a pad below the toe pads).

Bobcats have a white belly and a brown or pale-gray top with black spots. The tail usually has a black tip. They are mostly crepuscular (say it, cre-pus-cue-lar), which means they are most active in the dawn and twilight hours.

### Did you know?

Coyotes are the second-biggest group of large predators in Florida, aside from the American alligator (page 110). At one time, coyotes were only found in the central and western parts of the US, but now with the help of humans (eliminating predators and clearing forests), they can be found throughout most of the country.

Size Comparison    Most Active    Track Size

# Coyote
*Canis latrans*

**Size:** 3–4 feet long; weighs 21–50 pounds

**Habitat:** Urban and suburban areas, woodlands, grasslands, and farm fields

**Range:** Coyotes can be found in all the counties of Florida. They are also found throughout the US and Mexico, the northern parts of Central America, and in southern Canada.

**Food:** A variety of prey, including rodents, birds, deer, and sometimes livestock

**Den:** Coyotes will dig their own dens but will often use old fox or badger dens, or hollow logs.

**Young:** 5–7 pups, independent around 8–10 months

**Predators:** Bears and wolves; humans trap and kill for pelts and to "protect" livestock.

**Tracks:** Four toes and a carpal pad (the single pad below the toe pads) can be seen on all four feet.

Coyotes have a brown, reddish-brown, or gray back fur with a lighter gray to white belly. They have a longer muzzle than other wild canines. They are active mostly during the night (nocturnal) but also during the twilight and dawn hours (crepuscular).

### Did you know?

The eastern cottontail gets its name from its short, puffy tail that looks like a cotton ball. A cottontail can travel up to 18 miles per hour! Rabbits have great hearing and eyesight. They can almost see all the way around them (360 degrees). On days with high wind, they will bed down in a burrow because the wind interferes with their ability to hear and detect predators.

Size Comparison    Most Active    Track Size

3½"

# Eastern Cottontail

*Sylvilagus floridanus*

**Size:** 16–19 inches long; weighs 1½–4 pounds

**Habitat:** Forests, swamps, orchards, deserts, and farm areas

**Range:** Found throughout Florida; throughout the eastern US to Arizona and New Mexico; isolated ranges in the Pacific Northwest

**Food:** Clovers; grasses; wild strawberries; garden plants; and twigs of a variety of trees, including maple, oak, and sumac

**Den:** Rabbits don't dig dens; they bed in shallow, grassy, saucer-shaped depressions (holes) or under shrubs. They will sometimes use woodchuck dens in the winter.

**Young:** They usually have 2–4 kits at one time, but it's not uncommon to have 7 or more. Born naked and blind, they weigh about an ounce (about the same weight as a slice of bread) and gain weight very quickly.

**Predators:** Owls, coyotes, eagles, weasels, humans, and foxes

**Tracks:** The front foot is an inch long with four toe pads; the hind foot is 3½ inches long.

An eastern cottontail sports thick brown fur with a white belly, a gray rump, and a white "cotton" tail. During the winter, it survives by eating bark off of fruit trees and shrubs.

### Did you know?
The eastern fox squirrel's bones appear pink under ultraviolet (UV) light, a type of light human eyes can't see. Squirrels accidentally help plant trees by forgetting whey they previously buried nuts. Sometimes, they seem to pretend to bury nuts to throw off would-be nut thieves.

Size Comparison    Most Active    Track Size

2½"

# Eastern Fox Squirrel

*Sciurus niger*

**Size:** 19–28 inches long; weighs 1–3 pounds

**Habitat:** Open woodlands, suburban areas, and dense forests

**Range:** They are found throughout Florida and the eastern United States to Texas and as far north as the Dakotas.

**Food:** Acorns, seeds, nuts, insects such as moths and beetles, birds, eggs, and dead fish

**Den:** Ball-shaped dreys, or nests, are made of vegetation like leaves, sometimes in tree cavities.

**Young:** 2–3 kits are born between December and February and May and June. Kittens are born naked and weigh half an ounce; they are cared for by their parents for the first 7–8 weeks. They can reproduce by around 10–11 months for males and 8 months for females.

**Predators:** Humans, hawks, cats, coyotes, bobcats, and weasels

**Tracks:** The front tracks have four digits (toes), and the hind feet have five digits.

The eastern fox squirrel is the largest tree squirrel in Florida. It is gray or reddish brown with a yellowish or light-brown underside. There is also a black and smoky-gray color phase. Both the male and female look the same.

**Did you know?**

Moles are fossorial, meaning that they live most of their lives underground. One mole can tunnel about 60 feet in one day, which is equal to about 2½–3 school buses long. Due to their tunneling of dirt, they are seen as pests by some people. Others welcome their activity due to their aerating and turning the soil, as well as providing insect control of would-be nuisances to plant species.

Size Comparison    Most Active

# Eastern Mole

*Scalopus aquaticus*

**Size:** 5–7 inches long; weighs about 2½–5 ounces

**Habitat:** Open woodlands, fields, pastures, suburban areas, and meadows

**Range:** They are found throughout Florida and the eastern US to Texas and stretching northward into Minnesota.

**Food:** These carnivores eat earthworms, insects, and centipedes.

**Mating:** February to early April; males will search for mates in nearby tunnels.

**Den:** Nests are made of leaves, grasses, and other plant parts. They are usually made under logs, boulders, stumps, and clumps of grasses. Nests are at least 5 inches underground but can be 18 inches or more.

**Young:** 2–5 pups are born 40–45 days after mating. Pups are born with eyes closed, with no fur. They reach independent age around 4 weeks.

**Predators:** Snakes, foxes, coyotes, hawks, owls, domesticated cats and dogs, and humans

**Tracks:** Because moles live underground, their footprints are rare. Look for their tunnels and mounds.

Eastern moles are small, stocky, gray mammals. With their streamlined body design and robust forelimbs and claws, they are built for digging. They are gray to slate black with black hidden eyes; a buffy pink nose; and a short, naked tail.

**Did you know?**
Panthers are the second-largest cat in the Western Hemisphere.
The largest is the jaguar. Panthers do not roar like other big cats,
but rather they scream! They also make other sounds similar to
domesticated cats like hissing and purring.

Size Comparison     Most Active     Track Size

3"

# Florida Panther

*Puma concolor couguar*

**Size:** 6–8 feet long; weighs 100–160 pounds

**Habitat:** Grasslands, wetlands, shrublands, forests, swamps, and upland forests

**Range:** Florida panthers are primarily found in southwestern Florida.

**Food:** Carnivores; panthers eat mammals, birds, and occasionally livestock.

**Den:** Dens are lined with plants in caves, crevices, or thickets.

**Young:** 1–6 kittens are born almost 100 days after mating. Weaning takes place after around four months, and the young kits will stay with their mom another year or two. Males reach reproductive maturity at around 3 years and females around 2½ years.

**Predators:** No natural predators but will sometimes get in territory disputes with other large carnivores

**Tracks:** Front tracks are 3¼ inches long and wide. The back or hind tracks are 3 inches long and wide.

Panthers are the largest cat species found east of the Mississippi. Their fur is a golden tan to dusky brown on the back; the underside is a pale buff color with a white throat and chest area. They have a pink nose, black ear tips, yellow-brown eyes, and a smoky-gray-to-black muzzle. The tip of their tail is black, like their ears. The tail makes up a third of their body length. Kittens are spotted until they are 4–5 months old, and they have smoky-blue eyes.

### Did you know?
Gray foxes are the only member of the dog family in the US that can climb trees well. They have semi-retractable claws, almost like cats, enabling them to hang onto trees.

Size Comparison    Most Active    Track Size

1½"

# Gray Fox

*Urocyon cinereoargenteus*

**Size:** 2½–3½ feet long; weighs 6–10 pounds

**Habitat:** Forests, grasslands, urban (city) areas, and brushy and scrub-heavy areas near water sources

**Range:** Much of the continental United States; in Florida, they can be found statewide.

**Food:** Omnivorous (eating both plants and animals, including birds, insects, mice, and rabbits). Also eats apples, nuts, grasses, various berries, and corn

**Den:** Usually only dens during mating seasons. Sometimes they use abandoned dens of other animals that they will widen or extend; also uses hollowed-out trees and cavities, caves, and crevices in rocky areas.

**Young:** Kits or pups, sometimes called cubs, are born in April or May; litters of 4–5 young are born at one time; young feed on milk for approximately 3 weeks and are then fed solids. At around 4 months they learn to hunt, and they eventually leave the family around the 10-month mark.

**Predators:** Bobcats, great horned owls, coyotes, and humans

**Tracks:** Front paw is 1¾–2 inches long and 1¾ inches wide. Hind foot is 1½ inches long and 1¼–1¾ inches wide.

Males are a tad bit larger than females. Fur comes in various mixtures of reds, grays, white, and black. The breast, belly, and side areas are a brownish red. The head is salt-and-pepper (mixture of gray, white, and black) with a white muzzle or nose area, cheeks, and throat. The tail has a distinctive black stripe that runs to the tip and bushes out.

**Did you know?**
The Key deer is the smallest subspecies of white-tailed deer. Because of its size, it is sometimes called a "toy deer." Males grow to the size of a large dog (around 80 pounds). They get their name from the Florida Keys, the only area where they can be found.

Size Comparison

Most Active

Track Size
¾–1"

# Key Deer

*Odocoileus virginianus clavium*

**Size:** Male is 36 inches at shoulder height; female is 28 inches; male weighs 80 pounds; female weighs 65 pounds

**Habitat:** Mangroves (trees and shrubs growing on the coast), freshwater wetlands, pine forests, and woodlands

**Range:** Key deer are only found in Florida; they are only found in the Florida Keys.

**Food:** They are herbivores that eat a variety of plants; palm berries and several mangrove tree species are their favorites.

**Den:** Deer do not have dens but will bed down in tall grasses and shrub areas.

**Young:** Key deer are born about 200 days after mating between the months of April and June. One fawn is usually born a year, weighing 2–4 pounds at birth. Males will reach reproductive age around 1–1½ years but will usually not mate the first year. Females reach reproductive age at 6 months.

**Predators:** They have few natural predators due to location. Humans and dogs are the biggest threats.

**Tracks:** Similar to white-tailed deer but smaller

The Key deer's head and back are tan to dark brown. They have a white underside and a black nose. During the rut, or breeding season, males compete for females. After the rut, males lose their antlers, and new antlers start growing in over time.

### Did you know?

Manatees are nicknamed *sea cows* because, like cows, they are slow-moving plant eaters. They eat seagrasses and other aquatic plants. Manatees graze for 6–8 hours a day and consume over 5% of their body weight in plant material. They have a special top lip that aids them in eating. Like an elephant uses its trunk, manatees can use their lips to grab food.

Size Comparison    Most Active

# Manatee (West Indian Manatee)

*Trichechus manatus*

**Size:** 9–14 feet or longer; weighs 400–1,200 pounds

**Habitat:** Coastal wetland areas such as marshes, mangroves, river areas, and inland areas with natural springs

**Range:** Manatees can be found along the southeastern US coast, as well as along the coasts of some Central and South American countries. In Florida, they can be found along Florida's coastline. In the winter, they can be found throughout north and central Florida.

**Food:** Aquatic vegetation, like seagrass and eelgrass. Sometimes fish and invertebrates

**Den:** No den. Calves are born underwater, and the mom provides care.

**Young:** One calf is born at a time. Calves feed on milk for about 3 weeks and then transition to consuming plants. They depend on their mother for 2 years. Females reach reproductive maturity around 4 years but will usually breed at around 7–8 years. Males mature at around 9–10 years.

**Predators:** Due to their size and habitat, adult manatees do not have many natural predators other than humans. They suffer from boat collisions, fishing gear entanglement, and pollution. Young can sometimes fall prey to alligators and some species of sharks.

**Tracks:** They leave no tracks because they are in the water.

Manatees are gray to brownish gray. They are sparsely covered with hair on their body. Their nose area is covered with thick whiskers that they use to locate food and sense their environment. They have flippers and a paddle- or spoon-shaped tail.

### Did you know?

Mexican free-tailed bats are the fastest-known mammals on Earth, even faster than a cheetah at over 99 miles per hour (mph). A colony of Mexican free-tailed bats can consume over 250 tons of insects in a night; this makes them great at pest control for farmers. Sometimes they fly over 10,000 feet high. They get their name from the little section of tail that sticks out from their skin.

Size Comparison     Most Active

# Mexican Free-tailed Bat (Brazilian Free-tailed Bat)

*Tadarida brasiliensis*

**Size:** 3–4 inches long; wingspan is 11–12 inches; weighs ¼–½ ounce

**Habitat:** Wetland areas, caves, suburban areas, urban areas, forests, and deserts

**Range:** They are found across Florida, as well as throughout most of the southern half of the US.

**Food:** Carnivores; moths, beetles, flies, and dragonflies

**Den:** Roost sites are usually near water and in caves. In Florida, caves are limited and/or not ideal due to the humidity and temperature in the cave, as well as the amount of water inside. So human structures like bridges, abandoned buildings, and mines are used. Bats nest in colonies from as few as 40 bats to up to several thousand.

**Young:** One pup is born 11–12 weeks after mating. Pups roost in high areas where it is hot. Pups are raised by females. In about 4–7 weeks, they are independent. They can reproduce at around 9 months for females and 2 years for males.

**Predators:** Owls, hawks, skunks, opossums, raccoons, and snakes

**Tracks:** Though they are rarely on the ground to leave a track, it would show one thumbprint from the forearm and a hind footprint.

Mexican free-tailed bats are medium-size bats. They are dark brown to clay-red in color. They have large ears with black tips, a short nose, and wrinkled lips. They have long, narrow wings and a small, exposed tail.

The Mexican free-tailed bat does not often leave tracks.

**Did you know?**

The raccoon is great at catching fish and other aquatic animals, such as mussels and crawfish. They are also excellent swimmers but they apparently avoid swimming because the water makes their fur heavy. Raccoons can turn their feet 180 degrees; this helps them when climbing, especially when going head-first down trees.

Size Comparison      Most Active      Track Size      Hibernates

# Northern Raccoon

*Procyon lotor*

**Size:** 24–40 inches long; weighs 15–28 pounds

**Habitat:** Woody areas, grasslands, suburban and urban areas, wetlands, and marshes

**Range:** They are found throughout Florida and the US; they are also found in Mexico and southern Canada.

**Food:** Eggs, insects, garbage, garden plants, berries, nuts, fish, carrion, small mammals, and aquatic invertebrates like crawfish and mussels

**Den:** Raccoon dens are built in hollow trees, abandoned burrows, caves, and human-made structures.

**Young:** 2–6 young (kits) are born around March through July. They are born weighing 2 ounces, are around 4 inches long, and are blind with lightly colored fur.

**Predators:** Coyotes, foxes, bobcats, humans, and even large birds of prey

**Tracks:** Their front tracks resemble human handprints. The back tracks sort of look like human footprints.

The northern raccoon has dense fur with variations of brown, black, and white streaks. It has black, mask-like markings on its face and a black-and-gray/brownish ringed tail. During the fall, it will grow a thick layer of fat to aid in staying warm through the winter.

**Did you know?**
Otters are good swimmers and can close their nostrils while diving. This allows them to dive for as long as 8 minutes and to depths of over 50 feet. Otter fur is the thickest of all mammal fur. River otters have an incredible 67,000 hairs for every square centimeter!

Size Comparison    Most Active    Track Size

3"

# Northern River Otter

*Lontra canadensis*

**Size:** 29–48 inches long; weighs 10–33 pounds

**Habitat:** Lakes, marshes, rivers, and large streams; suburban areas

**Range:** Otters can be found throughout Florida, except for the Keys; they are found across much of the US, except parts of the Southwest and portions of the central US.

**Food:** Fish, frogs, snakes, crabs, crawfish, mussels, birds, eggs, turtles, and small mammals. They sometimes eat aquatic vegetation too.

**Den:** They den in burrows along the river, usually under rocks, riverbanks, hollow trees, and vegetation.

**Young:** 2–4 young (pups) are born between November and May. Pups are born with their eyes closed. They will leave the area at around 6 months old and reach full maturity at around 2 or 3 years.

**Predators:** Alligators, coyotes, bobcats, bears, and dogs

**Tracks:** Their feet have nonretractable claws and are webbed.

Northern river otters have thick, dark-brown fur and a long, slender body. Their fur is made up of two types: a short under-coat and a coarse top coat that repels water. They have webbed feet and a layer of fat that helps keep them warm in cold water.

**Did you know?**
The red fox is a great jumper and can leap over 13 feet in one bound. Red foxes are also fast, as they can run up to 30 miles per hour. Red foxes, like wild cats, will hide their food to eat later, often under leaf litter or in holes.

Size Comparison

Most Active

Track Size
2¼"

# Red Fox

*Vulpes vulpes*

**Size:** 37–42 inches long; weighs 8–15 pounds

**Habitat:** Grasslands, forest edges, farm fields, and suburban areas

**Range:** Foxes are common throughout much of the state; they can be found in nearly all of the US, except for the Southwest.

**Food:** Omnivores (they eat both meat and plants); they eat frogs, birds, snakes, small mammals, insects, seeds, nuts, and fruit.

**Den:** They dig underground dens, sometimes several at once, splitting a litter (babies) between the two. They also use old badger or groundhog holes or tree roots for den sites.

**Young:** 3–7 young (kits) are born; pups will nurse (drink milk from the mother) for around 10 weeks and will become independent at around 7 months.

**Predators:** Coyotes, lynx, cougars, and other species of carnivores. Humans trap and hunt foxes for fur.

**Tracks:** Their footprints resemble dog tracks, and have four toe pads; they walk in a line with the hind foot behind the front.

The red fox is a medium-size predator with a burnt orange or rust-like red coat with a bushy, white-tipped tail. The legs are usually black or grayish. The red fox's tail is about one third of its body length.

### Did you know?

The southeastern beach mouse is a subspecies of the oldfield mouse. Out of all the beach mice, the southeastern is the largest. Beach mice are important to the health of beaches due to their burrowing lifestyle. They eat insects that are pests to beach plants. The seeds that they eat help to spread important dune plants, and their burrowing helps to stimulate plant growth.

Size Comparison     Most Active     Track Size

¾"

# Southeastern Beach Mouse

*Peromyscus polionotus niveiventris*

**Size:** 5¼ inches long; weighs ⅖–½ ounce

**Habitat:** Coastal beaches, uplands, sand dunes, and coastal palmetto flats

**Range:** While the oldfield mouse is a resident commonly found in the southern states of Alabama, Georgia, and South Carolina, the southeastern beach mouse in Florida is restricted to the dunes of the Atlantic Coast in southern Volusia County to Martin County.

**Food:** Omnivores that feed on insects and vegetation, including beach grasses and sea oats

**Den:** Breeding activity happens November–January. Beach mice make their dens in underground burrows that they dig themselves.

**Young:** A litter of 4 pups is born 23 days after mating. Weaning takes place 18 days after birth, and the young mice will reach maturity at around 30 days.

**Predators:** Owls, coyotes, snakes, foxes, bobcats, and skunks

**Tracks:** ¼ inch wide by ½ inch long

Southeastern beach mice are small, pale rodents. The hair on their back is buff colored with a dark base of gray. The tail is buff colored on the top half of the tail, and the undertail is white.

## Did you know?

The southern flying squirrel doesn't actually fly! Instead, it uses special folds of skin to glide through the air. They can glide over 100 feet at a time. They have thick paws that aid them in landing. Because they move from tree to tree, they help to spread seeds and fungi.

Size Comparison    Most Active

# Southern Flying Squirrel

*Glaucomys volans*

**Size:** 9 inches long; weighs 2–3 ounces

**Habitat:** Forests with older trees

**Range:** They are found statewide in Florida and throughout the eastern US and parts of Mexico.

**Food:** Nuts, berries, acorns, small birds, mice, insects, and mushrooms

**Den:** They make nests in tree hollows. They will also use abandoned woodpecker holes and human-made nest boxes or birdhouses. They line the nest with chewed bark, grasses, moss, and feathers.

**Young:** 2–3 young (kits) are born per litter; they drink milk from the mother for around 70 days and will be fully independent around 4 months and mature at around a year old.

**Predators:** Small hawks, foxes, owls, martens (weasel-like mammals), and weasels

**Tracks:** Tracks are rare because they spend most of their time in trees.

The southern flying squirrel is a grayish-brown nocturnal (active at night) animal that glides through the air from tree to tree. The patagium, or skin fold, stretches from their ankles to their wrist, allowing them to "fly." (People have even built similar "squirrel suits" to glide with, and they've worked!) During winter months, flying squirrels share cavities with others.

### Did you know?

The spotted skunk is the only skunk in the US that can climb trees. Sometimes it will climb trees to knock down beehives and feed on the honeycombs. Skunks are most well-known for the oily, smelly substance that they can spray from their rear-end area. When spraying, they can usually hit what they're aiming for!

Size Comparison    Most Active    Track Size

1¼"

# Spotted Skunk

*Spilogale putorius*

**Size:** 16–24 inches long; weighs 1–4 pounds

**Habitat:** Forests, grasslands, shrublands, woodlands, and fields

**Range:** Found throughout much of Florida except pocket areas in the Keys and northeast areas of the state. They are found throughout much of the eastern United States and in areas of Canada and Mexico.

**Food:** Omnivore (eats both plants and animals); corn, rabbits, salamanders, insects, mice, fruit, birds, and bird eggs

**Den:** Dens are commonly made above the ground, in a hole or a rock crevice, or under a hollow log or stump. Will utilize multiple dens throughout home range for various purposes. While they can and will dig their own dens, they will also use abandoned dens made by other animals.

**Young:** Around 3–6 kits are born blind with the spotted black-and-white pattern. They are independent within 3 months and reach reproductive age around 11 months.

**Predators:** Owls, hawks, bobcats, and coyotes. Often injured by pet dogs

**Tracks:** Front feet are ¾ inch long and hind feet are 1¼ inches long. Both front and hind have five toe pads.

The spotted skunk is a small stocky animal with short legs. They have coarse, long fur that is patterned with black-and-white spots and stripes. They are smaller than the striped skunk.

## Did you know?

At one time the skunk was thought to have been part of the weasel family. Today it is classified as its own family, the Mephitidae. Skunks have a built-in self-defense mechanism; they have the ability to spray an oily chemical up to 20 feet to deter predators. During the wintertime, striped skunks can lose over half of their body weight.

Size Comparison  Most Active  Track Size  1½" Hibernates

# Striped Skunk

*Mephitis mephitis*

**Size:** 17–30 inches long; weighs 6–13 pounds

**Habitat:** Forests, grasslands, shrublands, suburban areas, woodlands, and fields

**Range:** Found throughout Florida except for the Keys, as well as much of the eastern United States and in Canada and Mexico

**Food:** Omnivore (eat both plants and animals); corn, rabbits, salamanders, insects, mice, fruit, fish, birds, and bird eggs

**Den:** Dens are usually cavities in a hole or a rock crevice, or under a hollow log or stump. The female will use grasses and weeds to build a nest.

**Young:** Around 3–6 kits are born blind with the striped black-and-white pattern. They are independent within 3 months and reach reproductive age around 10 months.

**Predators:** Owls, hawks, bobcats, foxes, eagles, and coyotes. Often injured by domesticated dogs

**Tracks:** Front feet are ⅞ inch long by 1⅛ inches wide, and hind feet are 1½ inches long by 1¾ inches wide. Both front and hind feet have 5 toe pads.

The striped skunk is larger than the spotted skunk. They have a coarse black coat with two white stripes that start at the head and flow down the back. They have a thinner white stripe that goes from the forehead to the tip of the nose. The stripe pattern is usually distinctive to each skunk.

### Did you know?

Tricolored bats got their name because of the three different colors of fur on their back: dark gray on the bottom, golden-brown in the middle, and brown or earth-tone red on the top. The tricolored bat is the smallest bat in Florida!

Size Comparison   Most Active   Hibernates

# Tricolored Bat

*Perimyotis subflavus*

**Size:** 3–3½ inches long; wingspan is 8⅓–10⅓ inches; weighs ⅒–¾ ounce or about as much as a quarter

**Habitat:** Forests, caves, urban (city) areas, grasslands, and orchards

**Range:** Widespread across the eastern and central US as far west as Texas. It can be found throughout Florida, except for the Keys.

**Food:** Mosquitoes, beetles, ants, moths, and cicadas

**Den:** Roost in trees, buildings, culverts (sewage drains), caves, and in Spanish moss. Females will roost in colonies of 25 or more individuals. Males are solitary and do not have bachelor colonies like other bat species. Bats mate in the fall and give birth in the spring.

**Young:** Pups are born blind and furless in June and July. Pups learn to fly 3 weeks after birth, and within a month they are able to hunt for themselves. They are mature by their first fall but will not usually mate until their second fall.

**Predators:** Owls, raccoons, snakes, and hawks

**Tracks:** Though they are rarely on the ground to leave a track, it would show as one thumbprint from the forearm and a hind footprint.

Tricolored bats are a golden hue of yellowish and brown fur. Single hairs are darkly shaded at the bottom, yellow hued in the midsection, and brown at the tip. This is the reason for the name "tricolored." During the winter they hibernate in caves, mines, and rock crevices. In areas with a lack of caves or mines, they hibernate in roadside culverts.

The tricolored bat does not often leave tracks.

## Did you know?

The opossum is the only marsupial native to the US. Marsupials are a special group of animals that are most well-known for their pouches, which they use to carry their young. When frightened, young opossums will play dead (called playing possum) and adults will show their teeth and hiss or run away.

Size Comparison    Most Active    Track Size

2½"

# Virginia Opossum

*Didelphis virginiana*

**Size:** 22–45 inches long; weighs 4–8 pounds

**Habitat:** Forests, woodlands, meadows, and suburban areas

**Range:** They are found throughout Florida; they are found throughout the eastern US, Canada, and also in Mexico and Costa Rica.

**Food:** Eggs, small mammals, garbage, insects, worms, birds, fruit, and occasionally small reptiles and amphibians

**Den:** They den in hollow trees, abandoned animal burrows, and buildings.

**Young:** A litter of 6–20 young (joeys) are born blind and without fur; their limbs are not fully formed. Young will climb from the birthing area into the mother's pouch and stay until 8 weeks old; they then alternate between the mother's pouch and her back for 4 weeks. At 12 weeks they are independent.

**Predators:** Hawks, owls, pet cats and dogs, coyotes, and bobcats

**Tracks:** The front feet are 2 inches long and around 1½ inches wide and resemble a child's hands; the hind feet are 2½ inches long and around 2¼ inches wide; they have fingers in front with a fifth finger that acts as a thumb.

The Virginia opossum has long gray-and-black fur; the face is white, and the tail is pink to gray and furless. Opossums have long claws.

53

## Did you know?

When they first emerge, a deer's antlers are covered in a special skin called velvet. Deer can run up to 40 miles per hour and can jump over 8 feet vertically (high) and over 15 feet horizontally (across).

Size Comparison    Most Active    Track Size

3"

# White-tailed Deer

*Odocoileus virginianus*

**Size:** 4–6 feet long; 3–4 feet tall at front shoulder; weighs 114–308 pounds

**Habitat:** Forest edges, brushy fields, wooded farmlands, prairies, and swamps

**Range:** They are found throughout Florida and throughout the US except for much of the Southwest; they are also found in southern Canada and into South America.

**Food:** Fruits, grass, tree shrubs, nuts, and bark

**Den:** Deer do not den but will bed down in tall grasses and shrubby areas.

**Young:** Deer usually give birth to twins (fawns) that are 3–6 pounds in late May to June. The fawns are born with spots; this coloration helps them hide in vegetation. Young become independent at 1–2 years.

**Predators:** Wolves, coyotes, bears, bobcats, and humans

**Tracks:** Both front and hind feet have two teardrop- or comma-shaped toes.

Crepuscular (active at dawn and dusk), white-tailed deer have big brown eyes with eye rings and a long snout with a black, glossy nose. The males have antlers, which fall off each year. All deer have a white tail that they flash upward when alarmed. Deer molt or change fur color twice a year. They sport rusty-brown fur in the summer; in early fall, they transition to winter coats that are grayish brown in color.

**Did you know?**
The American goldfinch helps restore habitats by spreading seeds. The goldfinch gets its color from a pigment called a carotenoid (say it, cuh-rot-en-oid) in the seeds it eats. It can even feed upside down by using its feet to bring seeds to its mouth.

Nest Type

# American Goldfinch

*Spinus tristis*

**Size:** 4½–5 inches long; wingspan of 9 inches; weighs about half an ounce

**Habitat:** Grasslands, meadows, suburban areas, and wetlands

**Range:** Found throughout Florida in winter

**Food:** Seeds of plants and trees; sometimes feeds on insects; loves thistle seeds at birdfeeders

**Nesting:** Goldfinches build nests in late June.

**Nest:** Cup-shaped nests are built a couple of feet aboveground out of roots and plant fibers.

**Eggs:** 2–7 eggs with a bluish-white tint

**Young:** Young (chicks) hatch around 15 days after being laid; they hatch without feathers and weigh only a gram. Chicks learn to fly after around 11–15 days. Young become mature at around 11 months old.

**Predators:** Garter snakes, blue jays, American kestrels, and cats

**Migration:** Can be seen across much of North America; in Florida they are found statewide in winter.

During the summer, American goldfinch males are brightly colored with golden-yellow feathers and an orange beak. They have black wings with white wing bars. The crown (top) of the head is black. In winter, they molt, and the males look more like the females. Females are always greenish yellow with hints of yellow around the head.

### Did you know?

Anhingas often soar high up in the sky in groups called "kettles," often with raptors. The anhinga is less buoyant (floats less easily) than other birds, so its body sits lower in the water with its head and neck sticking out, making it easy to mistake for a snake. This is why it is sometimes called the snake bird.

Nest Type     Migrates

# Anhinga
*Anhinga anhinga*

**Size:** 28½–37½ inches long; wingspan of 43 inches; weighs 45–48 ounces

**Habitat:** Shallow areas of freshwater marshes, swamps, mangroves, lagoons, and rivers

**Range:** Can be found year-round in the eastern coastal areas of the US. In Florida, they are year-round residents.

**Food:** Mostly fish, but they also feed on aquatic (water-living) insects, crawfish, and shrimp. Sometimes they will take on snakes, alligator hatchlings, and baby turtles.

**Nesting:** Nesting takes place in colonies, or rookeries, of other water-loving birds. Parents share care duties.

**Nest:** Platform nests are constructed mostly by the female with the male supplying sticks and twigs; the inside is usually lined with grasses and leaves.

**Eggs:** 2–5 palish-white-to-blue eggs about 2–2½ inches long and 1½ inches wide

**Young:** Eggs hatch 25–30 days after laying. Chicks are born with eyes open and featherless. Young will leap out of the nest in the presence of danger.

**Predators:** Snakes, squirrels, owls, common ravens, blue jays, red-bellied woodpeckers, and a variety of hawks

**Migration:** Most are year-round residents that will migrate short distances to areas in Florida or Mexico.

Males are black with whitish to silver streaking on the back and wings. Juveniles and females have a light-brown-to-tan head and body. Both sexes have orange-yellow feet, legs, and bill.

### Did you know?

The bald eagle is an endangered species success story! The bald eagle was once endangered due to a pesticide called DDT that weakened eggshells and caused them to crack early. Through the banning of DDT and other conservation efforts, the bald eagle population recovered, and it was removed from the Endangered Species List in July of 2007.

Nest Type

Migrates

# Bald Eagle

*Haliaeetus leucocephalus*

**Size:** 3½ feet long; wingspan of 6½–8 feet; weighs 8–14 pounds

**Habitat:** Forests and tree stands (small forests) near river edges, lakes, seashores, and wetlands

**Range:** They are a resident bird throughout Florida; they are found throughout much of the US.

**Food:** Fish, waterfowl (ducks), rabbits, squirrels, muskrats, and deer carcasses; will steal food from other eagles or osprey

**Nesting:** Eagles have lifelong partners that begin nesting in fall, laying eggs between November–February.

**Nest:** They build a large nest out of sticks, high up in trees; the nest can be over 5 feet wide and over 6 feet tall, often shaped like an upside-down cone.

**Eggs:** 1–3 white eggs

**Young:** Young (chicks) will hatch around 35 days; young will leave the nest around 12 weeks. It takes up to 5 years for eagles to get that iconic look!

**Predators:** Few; collisions with cars sometimes occur.

**Migration:** They are short-distance migrators, usually to coastal areas; in Florida, many eagles do not migrate at all.

Adult bald eagles have a dark-brown body, a white head and tail, and a golden-yellow beak. Juvenile eagles are mostly brown at first, but their color pattern changes over their first few years. A bald eagle can use its wings as oars to propel itself across bodies of water.

**61**

**Did you know?**
The barred owl has dark brown eyes; many other owls have yellow eyes. Barred owls, like other owls, have special structures on their primary feathers that allow them to fly silently through the air.

Nest Type

# Barred Owl

*Strix varia*

**Size:** 17–20 inches long; wingspan of 3½ feet; weighs 2 pounds

**Habitat:** Forested areas, near floodplains of lakes and rivers

**Range:** They can be found throughout the state of Florida; they are found throughout the eastern US and southern Canada, with scattered populations throughout the Pacific Northwest.

**Food:** Squirrels, rabbits, and mice; will also prey on birds and aquatic animals like frogs, fish, and crawfish

**Nesting:** Courtship starts in late fall; nesting starts in winter

**Nest:** They use hollow trees; they will also use abandoned nests of other animals and human-made nest structures.

**Eggs:** 2–4 white eggs with a rough shell

**Young:** Young (chicks) hatch between 27 and 33 days; they have white down feathers and leave the nest around 5 weeks after hatching. They are fully independent at around 6 months and fully mature at around 2 years.

**Predators:** Great horned owls, raccoons, weasels, and sometimes northern goshawks feed on eggs and young in the nest.

**Migration:** Barred owls do not migrate.

The barred owl is a medium-size bird with dark rings highlighting the face. Their feathers are brown and grayish, often with streaking or a bar-like pattern. They have no ear tufts and have a rounded head with a yellow beak and brown eyes. They can easily be identified by their call: "Who cooks for you, who cooks for you all?"

**Did you know?**
Kingfishers inspired human technology! Bullet trains around the world are designed after the kingfisher's beak, which allows them to dive into water without a splash. This design was used in bullet trains to allow them to enter into tunnels without making a large booming sound. This process of modeling human technology after animal features is called biomimicry.

Nest Type

Migrates

# Belted Kingfisher

*Megaceryle alcyon*

**Size:** 11–13¾ inches long; wingspan is 19–24 inches; weighs 5–6 ounces

**Habitat:** Forests and grassland areas near rivers, ponds, lakes

**Range:** Year-round resident that can be found throughout much of Florida as well as most of the United States; in other areas of the US and Canada.

**Food:** Mostly carnivorous; mostly fish and other aquatic animals such as crawfish and frogs, and occasionally other birds, mammals, and berries

**Nesting:** Nests are in the form of upward-sloped burrows that are dug in soft banks on or near water. (The upward slopes prevent flooding.)

**Nest:** Females and males select the nest site together; male does most of the digging.

**Eggs:** 5–8 white, smooth, glossy eggs are laid per clutch (group of eggs).

**Young:** Chicks are born featherless with pink skin, closed eyes, and a dark bill. They receive care from both parents. Chicks leave the nest after about 28 days.

**Predators:** Snakes, hawks, and mammals

**Migration:** Mostly a resident bird; in some areas, will migrate south during nonbreeding season

The belted kingfisher is bluish gray on top; the bottom half is white with a blue/gray belt or band. The wings have white spots on them. Unlike most other birds, the kingfisher female has a different pattern than the male. Females have a second reddish-brown or rusty-orange band on their belly.

**Did you know?**
Turkey vultures have something most birds don't: a good sense of smell. Black vultures take advantage of this by soaring in circles above a turkey vulture and waiting until it finds food. Then they join in on the meal. A trick to tell them apart: Black vultures are all black with white wing tips. Turkey vultures make a black "T" shape and have light gray undersides on the wings/tail.

# Black Vulture/Turkey Vulture

*Coragyps atratus/Cathartes aura*

**Size:** Black: 23½–27 inches long; wingspan is 53½–59 inches; weighs 56½–78 ounces. Turkey: 25¼–32 inches long; wingspan is 66–70 inches; weighs 70 ounces

**Habitat:** Forests, woodland edges, cities, farmland

**Range:** Year-round in Florida

**Food:** Carrion (dead animals) like deer, snakes, feral hogs, coyotes, and armadillos. Black vultures may kill smaller animals if given the chance.

**Nesting:** Black: Caves, tree cavities, brush piles, abandoned buildings in large groups. Turkey: Secluded caves, cliff ledges, hollow trees, abandoned nests

**Nest:** Black: Existing cavities in nature. Turkey: A simple "scrape" nest of discarded plants or wood

**Eggs:** Black: 1–3 speckled white eggs; Turkey: 1–3 creamy-white, speckled eggs

**Young:** Black: Chicks fledge after 10 weeks but depend on their parents for several months. Turkey: Chicks fledge 70 days after hatching and are independent a week or so afterward.

**Predators:** Raccoons, opossums, and foxes prey on eggs. Snakes, eagles, hawks, and owls may attack juveniles or sick or injured adults. Healthy adults are rarely prey.

**Migration:** Black: May migrate short distances. Turkey: Those in the northern US migrate south.

Black vultures are all black with white wing tips. Turkey vultures look all black, but up close, they are different shades of light gray and brown. Turkey vultures have a red head.

**Did you know?**
A medium-size songbird, blue grosbeaks belong to the same family as northern cardinals. Blue grosbeaks will sometimes add snakeskin to their nest, which is believed to help ward off predators.

Nest Type

Migrates

# Blue Grosbeak

*Passerina caerulea*

**Size:** 5½–6½ inches long; wingspan of 10¼–11½ inches; weighs 1–1¼ ounces

**Habitat:** Edges of woodlands, scrubs, farmlands, suburban and urban areas, overgrown fields, and thickets

**Range:** Throughout Florida during breeding and migration season

**Food:** Omnivores; insects, snails, spiders, as well as seeds

**Nesting:** April–August; along roadside and open areas

**Nest:** Nest is usually built by the female in dense, low vegetation usually 3–10 feet off the ground. An open cup nest is made of weeds, twigs, leaves, bark, and human-made material. Sometimes, snakeskin is also used. Nest is lined with grass and animal hair.

**Eggs:** Female lays 3–5 pale blue-to-white eggs. Eggs are just under an inch long and about ½–¾ inch wide. Females may lay 2 broods a year.

**Young:** Chicks hatch about 11–12 days after laying. They fledge (leave nest) around day 9–10. Chicks sometimes will continue being fed by the male, especially if the female has a second nest.

**Predators:** Snakes, domestic cats, and raptors. Brown-headed cowbirds often lay eggs in blue grosbeak nests.

**Migration:** Migrates to the Caribbean, Central America, and Mexico

The female is duller than the male, sporting a majority golden-brown plumage with a mix of faded blue feathers woven in. The male is bright blue with wing bars of black and brown. The male also has a small black mask adorned just behind his beak.

## Did you know?

Brown pelicans are the only species of pelican in the United States that dives from the sky to catch food. Sometimes they dive from over 55 feet above the water. The pelican's beak system (beak and pouch) can hold an incredible amount of water, up to 3 gallons, and lots of fish!

Nest Type

# Brown Pelican

*Pelecanus occidentalis*

**Size:** 41½–54 inches long; wingspan of 5¾–6½ feet; weighs 5¾–12 pounds

**Habitat:** Estuaries, coastal and inland areas, mangroves

**Range:** Brown pelicans can be found along much of North America's coast. Found throughout coastal Florida

**Food:** Carnivores that mostly eat fish, as well as amphibians, eggs, crustaceans, and other birds

**Nesting:** Winter-summer, depending on location.

**Nest:** The male selects the nest site and the female builds the nest on the ground or in trees. Nests on the ground are usually depressions or scrapes that are lined with plants. Nests in trees are usually platforms made of sticks lined with plants. Nesting takes places in colonies with other seabirds.

**Eggs:** 1 brood of 2–4 chalky- or milky-white eggs

**Young:** Both parents incubate the nest for 28–30 days. Young fledge around 63–75 days, taking longer to fledge. Birds are mature after 3-4 years.

**Predators:** Brown Pelicans have no natural predators, but sometimes chicks and eggs are predated by gulls, skunks, raccoons, and domestic dogs and cats.

**Migration:** In much of their range, including in Florida, they don't migrate.

Juvenile pelicans are mostly brown. In breeding season, adults are mostly brown with a white head with a pale–medium yellow hue on top and pink skin around the eyes. The neck area is dark burgundy with the sides of the neck having white lines that outline the pelican's gular pouch (the flap on the beak). The nonbreeding adults are more drab. The female is smaller than the male.

### Did you know?

Burrowing owls are fossorial, meaning that they live and/or spend most of their day underground. They will sometimes mimic rattlesnakes when threatened, by hiding in a burrow and making rattling and hissing sounds. They like to decorate their mounds with scat, or poop, from mammals. It is believed that the scat helps to attract insects to eat and to hide the scent of the owl's young.

Nest Type

# Burrowing Owl

*Athene cunicularia*

**Size:** 7½–11 inches long; wingspan of 20–22 inches; weighs 5–6 ounces

**Habitat:** Savanna forest, urban and suburban areas, farmlands, shrublands, prairies, deserts, and mountains

**Range:** There are populations found throughout peninsular Florida

**Food:** Carnivores; mostly insects and rodents, but also amphibians, reptiles, birds, and rarely seeds and fruit

**Nesting:** March–April

**Nest:** Nests are located in burrows usually made by other animals. In Florida, they usually make the burrows themselves. The male will line the nesting burrow with plants, feathers, scat, and sometimes trash.

**Eggs:** 4–12 white eggs often tinted the color of the dirt

**Young:** Owlets hatch 3–4 weeks after laying, covered with down that is gray or white. Within 4 weeks, they are able to fly short distances and explore areas outside of the burrow. They will receive care for another 1 to 3 months until they can hunt.

**Predators:** Snakes, domestic cats and dogs, foxes, skunks, hawks, falcons, weasels, and other species of owl; humans play a heavy role in displacement and loss of habitat.

**Migration:** Florida populations do not migrate.

Burrowing owls are small, brown owls adorned by white spots of various sizes on their back. They have a white or creamy belly with brown bars. They have large yellow eyes with thick white eyebrows and throat.

### Did you know?

The great blue heron is the largest and most common heron species. A heron's eye color changes as it ages. The eyes start out gray but transition to yellow over time. Great blue herons swallow their prey whole.

Nest Type

Migrates

# Great Blue Heron

*Ardea herodias*

**Size:** 3–4½ feet long; wingspan of 6–7 feet; weighs 5–7 pounds

**Habitat:** Lakes, ponds, rivers, marshes, lagoons, wetlands, and coastal areas like beaches

**Range:** They can be found throughout Florida, as well as the entirety of the United States and down into Mexico.

**Food:** Fish, rats, crabs, shrimp, grasshoppers, crawfish, other birds, small mammals, snakes, and lizards

**Nesting:** May to August

**Nest:** 2–3 feet across and saucer shaped; often grouped in large rookeries (colonies) in tall trees along the water's edge. Nests are built out of sticks and are often located in dead trees more than 100 feet above the ground; nests are used year after year.

**Eggs:** 3–7 pale bluish eggs

**Young:** Chicks will hatch after 28 days of incubation; young will stay in the nest for around 10 weeks. They reach reproductive maturity at just under 2 years.

**Predators:** Eagles, crows, gulls, raccoons, bears, and hawks

**Migration:** Populations in northern areas will fly south to southern states, the Caribbean, and Central America.

The great blue heron is a large wading bird with blue and gray upper body feathers; the belly area is white. They have long yellow legs that they use to stalk prey in the water. Great blue herons are famous for stalking prey at the water's edge; their specially adapted feet keep them from sinking into the mud!

**Did you know?**
Magnificent frigatebirds are seabirds, but their feathers are not waterproof. They have perfected techniques that allow them to catch prey without touching the water. One method is catching animals, such as flying fish, out of the air.

Nest Type

# Magnificent Frigatebird

*Fregata magnificens*

**Size:** 35–45 inches long; wingspan of 85½–90 inches; weighs 2¼–3½ pounds

**Habitat:** Open ocean and coastal areas

**Range:** Can be seen throughout the waters around northern Mexico and off the coast of Ecuador. In the Atlantic, they can be seen between Florida and Brazil. In Florida, they frequent the coastal areas of the state.

**Food:** Marine organisms like squid, fish, and crustaceans. Occasionally eats turtles, eggs, and bird chicks

**Nesting:** December–April. Males will mate every year. Females mate every other year. Males inflate the large red throat sac to attract a mate.

**Nest:** Males will bring sticks to the female to make a platform nest. Sometimes the sticks are stolen from other males. Nests are roughly 14 inches wide. The nest is never left unguarded until young are half grown.

**Eggs:** One white egg about 2½ inches long by 1¾ inches

**Young:** After 55 days or so, a chick will hatch naked and unable to take care of itself. Both parents take care of the chick at first, but the male leaves after about 2 months. The chick fledges around 6 months, but it will receive care for up to 4 more months from mom.

**Predators:** House cats prey upon eggs and chicks

**Migration:** In Florida, they do not migrate.

The magnificent frigatebird is a large seabird with black feathers. The females are larger than the males and have a white breast and underside. Both sexes have a long, forked tail and large wings. They have a large, hooked bill.

### Did you know?

When viewed straight-on, the yellow portion on the mallard's bill resembles a cartoon dog's head. Most domesticated ducks share the mallard as their ancestor. mallard feathers are waterproof; they use oil from the preen gland beneath their feathers to help aid in repelling water. Mallards are the most common duck in the United States and Florida.

Nest Type

Migrates

# Mallard

*Anas platyrhynchos*

**Size:** 24 inches long; wingspan of 36 inches; weighs 2½–3 pounds

**Habitat:** Lakes, ponds, rivers, and marshes

**Range:** They are found throughout Florida; the population stretches across the United States and Canada into Mexico and as far up as central Alaska.

**Food:** Insects, worms, snails, aquatic vegetation, sedge seeds, grasses, snails, and wild rice

**Nesting:** April to August

**Nest:** The nest is constructed on the ground, usually near a body of water.

**Eggs:** 9–13 eggs

**Young:** Eggs hatch 26–28 days after being laid. The ducklings are fully feathered and have the ability to swim at the time of hatching. Ducklings are cared for until they're 2–3 months old and reach reproductive maturity at 1 year old.

**Predators:** Humans, crows, mink, coyotes, raccoons, and snapping turtles

**Migration:** After breeding season, a lot of the population will migrate south; others will stay in familiar areas that have adequate food and shelter.

Male mallards are gray with an iridescent green head with a tinge of purple spotting, a white line along the collar, rusty-brown chest, yellow bill, and orange legs and feet. Females are dull brown with a yellow bill, a bluish area near the tail, and orange feet.

### Did you know?

Kites are considered raptors. Mississippi and swallow-tailed kites will eat on the wing, meaning they catch their food and eat it while flying. Kites are social and will hunt and roost in groups. Mississippi kites will purposely build nests near bees and wasps to aid in protecting the chicks from bot flies. Swallow-tailed kites drink by skimming the surface of the water and collecting it in their beak.

Nest Type

Migrates

# Mississippi Kite (MK)/ Swallow-tailed Kite (SK)

*Ictinia mississippiensis/ Elanoides forficatus*

**Size:** MK: 11¾–13¾ inches long; wingspan of 36 inches; weighs 7½–13¾ ounces. SK: 19¾–27 inches long; wingspan of 36 inches; weighs 11–21 ounces

**Habitat:** MK: Forests, suburban, and urban areas, prairies. SK: Wetlands, farm fields, coast, forests

**Range:** MK: During the breeding season, they can be found across the southern US, including the Panhandle and a small portion of northern Florida. SK: During breeding seasons, they can be seen from east Texas to South Carolina. Seen throughout Florida

**Food:** MK: Carnivores; mainly insects but will also eat small animals like birds, amphibians, reptiles, and small mammals. SK: Carnivores; flying insects, frogs, snakes, fish, fruit, and lizards

**Nesting:** MK: May to June, in colonies. SK: March to May

**Nest:** MK: Both sexes build a platform 20–30 feet off the ground. SK: Built by both sexes in trees.

**Eggs:** MK: 1–2 bluish-white eggs. SK: 1–3 cream-colored eggs

**Young:** MK: Chicks hatch 29–31 days; learn to fly around 5 weeks and fledge around 8 weeks. SK: Chicks hatch at around a month; learn to fly around 5 weeks.

**Predators:** MK: Ravens, owls, raccoons. SK: Owls, hawks

**Migration:** Migrate and spend the winter in South America

The Mississippi kite comes in various shades of gray, with red eyes and red to yellow legs. The Swallow-tailed kite has black wings, feet, bill, and forked tail. The rest of the body is gray.

**Did you know?**
Cardinals are very territorial and will sometimes attack their own reflection thinking that another cardinal has entered its territory. The early bird gets the worm, and cardinals are some of the first birds active in the morning.

Nest Type

# Northern Cardinal

*Cardinalis cardinalis*

**Size:** 8–9 inches long; wingspan of 12 inches

**Habitat:** Hardwood forests, urban areas, orchards, backyards, and fields

**Range:** They are found throughout Florida, as well as the eastern and midwestern parts of the United States.

**Food:** Seeds, fruits, insects, spiders, and centipedes

**Nesting:** March to August

**Nest:** The cup-shaped nest is built by females in thick foliage, usually at least 1 foot off the ground. It can be 3 inches tall and 4 inches wide.

**Eggs:** The female lays 2–5 off-white eggs with a variety of colored speckles

**Young:** About 2 weeks after eggs are laid, chicks hatch with their eyes closed and mostly naked, aside from sparsely placed down feathers.

**Predators:** Hawks, owls, and squirrels

**Migration:** Cardinals do not migrate.

Northern cardinal males are bright-red birds with a black face. Females are a washed-out red or brown. Both males and females have a crest (tuft of feathers on the head), and orange beaks and grayish legs. Cardinals can be identified by their laser-gun-like call.

**Did you know?**
The osprey is nicknamed the "fish hawk" because it is the only hawk in North America that mainly eats live fish. An osprey will rotate its catch to put it in line with its body, pointing head first, which allows for less resistance in flight as the air travels over the fish.

Nest Type

Migrates

# Osprey
*Pandion haliaetus*

**Size:** 21–23 inches long; wingspan of 59–71 inches; weighs 3–4½ pounds

**Habitat:** Near lakes, ponds, rivers, swamps, and reservoirs

**Range:** Resident for most of Florida with small area where they are only overwintering. Throughout the US.

**Food:** Feeds mostly on fish; they sometimes eat mammals, birds, and reptiles if there are few fish.

**Nesting:** For ospreys that migrate, egg-laying happens in April and May. The female will take on most of the incubation of the eggs, as well as the jobs of keeping the offspring warm and providing protection.

**Nest:** Platform nests are constructed out of twigs and sticks. Nests are constructed on trees, snags, or human-made objects like cellular towers and telephone poles.

**Eggs:** The mother lays 1–3 cream-colored eggs; they have splotches of various shades of brown and pinkish red on them.

**Young:** Chicks hatch after around 36 days and have brown-and-white down feathers. Osprey fledge around 50–55 days after hatching and will receive care from parents for another 2 months or so.

**Predators:** Owls, eagles, foxes, skunks, raccoons, snakes

**Migration:** Ospreys migrate south to wintering areas in the fall.

Ospreys are raptors, and they have a brown upper body and white lower body. The wings are brown on the outside and white on the underside with brown spotting and streaks towards the edge. The head is white with a brown band that goes through the eye area, highlighting the yellow eyes.

**Did you know?**

Painted buntings are the only birds in the United States that have a solid red breast and belly, and a solid blue head. Males do not get their iconic plumage until after their second year. Sometimes painted buntings will steal prey from spiders and their webs.

Nest Type

Migrates

# Painted Bunting

*Passerina ciris*

**Size:** 5½ inches long; wingspan of 8¾ inches; weighs ½ ounce

**Habitat:** Hardwood forests, urban areas, orchards, coastal areas, backyards, and fields

**Range:** Found throughout Florida during the breeding and nonbreeding seasons, as well as the eastern and mid-western US.

**Food:** Omnivores; diet depends on the season. They feed on seeds, snails, insects, spiders, and caterpillars.

**Nesting:** March to early August. Males arrive first and pick a breeding area to defend. Both birds pick a nesting area.

**Nest:** The cup-shaped nest is built by females in thick foliage at least 3–6 feet off the ground. It can be 2½ inches tall and 3 inches wide. The nest is woven out of leaves, bark, twigs, spiderwebs, and grasses. It is lined with grasses and hair.

**Eggs:** 3–4 gray or blue-white eggs with brown or gray spots.

**Young:** Chicks hatch 12 days after eggs are laid; they are born mostly naked, with eyes closed. Both parents feed the young. The chicks fledge around day 12 but will receive care for at least 3 more weeks. Females may raise two broods a year.

**Predators:** Hawks, owls, and squirrels

**Migration:** They migrate at night to warmer areas in fall.

Male painted buntings are a brightly colored mix of blues, greens, reds, and yellows. Females and juveniles are dullish or semi-bright yellow to olive green with eye rings.

**Did you know?**

The peregrine falcon is the fastest diving bird in the world. A peregrine falcon can reach speeds over 200 miles per hour (mph) when diving. To aid in diving and maneuvering in the air, like most other birds, peregrine falcons have a third eyelid called a nictitating membrane that helps to keep out debris and wind.

# Peregrine Falcon

*Falco peregrinus*

**Size:** 14–19½ inches long; wingspan of 39–43 inches; weighs 1–3½ pounds

**Habitat:** Hardwood forests, coastal areas and marshes, urban areas, orchards, backyards, and fields

**Range:** They are found throughout much of Florida as nonbreeding residents. Peregrine Falcons can be found throughout North America.

**Food:** Carnivores, feeding on pigeons, songbirds, aquatic birds, rodents, and sometimes bats

**Nesting:** February to March. Pairs mate for life and reuse nests. The female chooses a nest site and will scrape a shallow hole in loose soil or sand. Nests are usually on cliff edges or tall buildings. Sometimes they even use abandoned nests of other large birds.

**Nest:** Shallow ground scrapes about 8–9 inches wide and 2 inches deep with no extra nesting materials added.

**Eggs:** 3–5 off-white-to-brown eggs speckled brown or purple

**Young:** 30 days after eggs are laid, chicks (or eyas) will hatch with eyes closed and covered in off-white down.

**Predators:** Great horned owls, golden eagles, and humans

**Migration:** Northern and central populations migrate for breeding. Coastal populations are less likely to migrate.

The female is slightly larger than the male. Peregrine falcons have gray wings with black to gray bar-like marks and deep black wing tips. The breast and belly areas are covered with black-to-brown horizontal streaks or bars. They have a black head and black head and black marks below the eyes. The neck is white. The beak, legs, eye rings, and feet are yellow.

**Did you know?**
The red-tailed hawk is the most abundant hawk in North America. (Look for it on powerlines!) The red-tailed hawk's scream is the sound effect that you hear when soaring eagles are shown in movies. Eagles do not screech like hawks, so filmmakers use hawk calls instead!

Nest Type

Migrates

# Red-tailed Hawk (RT)/ Red-shouldered Hawk (RS)

*Buteo jamaicensis / Buteo lineatus*

**Size:** RT: 19–25 inches long; wingspan of 47–57 inches; weighs 2½–4 pounds. RS: 16½–24 inches long; wingspan of 37–43 inches; weighs around 1 pound

**Habitat:** RT: Deserts, woodlands, fields. RS: Forests, swamps, grasslands, urban areas

**Range:** RT: Florida and throughout North America. RS: Found throughout Florida and the eastern US; also found on parts of the Pacific Coast

**Food:** RT: Rodents, birds, reptiles, bats, and insects. RS: Small mammals, lizards, snakes, crawfish, songbirds

**Nesting:** Hawks mate for life; nesting starts in March.

**Nest:** RT: Both parents build a large cup-shaped nest (can be 6 feet high and 3 feet wide), made of sticks and branches. RS: Both male and female build a cup-shaped nest 20 feet off the ground.

**Eggs:** RT: White with colored blotches; RS: Off-white or slightly blue with varied markings

**Young:** RT: Young hatch after 30 days. They can fly at 5–6 weeks. RS: Chicks can fly after 5–6 weeks.

**Predators:** RT: Owls and crows. RS: Snakes, mammals, and owls

**Migration:** Birds in the northern areas of range will migrate short distances to warmer areas, while the hawks in the southern part of the state do not migrate.

Red-tailed hawks are named for their rusty-red tails! They have brown heads and a creamy, light-brown chest with a band of brown streaks. Red-shouldered hawks have a reddish-brown head and back, rusty undersides, and white barring on the belly. **91**

**Did you know?**
Spoonbills have feathers on their head until they reach maturity around 3 years or so; that's when they get the iconic bald head. Spoonbills also hatch with a straight bill, which later changes to the famous spoon-like shape as they get older. Their nostrils are located high up on their bill, near the eyes. This enables them to breathe while the rest of the bill is underwater.

Nest Type

# Roseate Spoonbill

*Platalea ajaja*

**Size:** 28–34 inches long; wingspan of 47–50 inches; weighs 2½–4 pounds

**Habitat:** Shrubby coastal areas, marshes, bays, swamps, mangroves, and mudflats

**Range:** Found throughout Florida and southeastern US coasts

**Food:** Mostly carnivorous; feeds on crustaceans, shrimp, aquatic insects, amphibians, and smaller fish

**Nesting:** Nesting takes place in trees and shrubs near water in colonies with other wading birds.

**Nest:** Large and cup shaped, made of branches and stems. Males collect the nest material and the females build the nest in high, shady areas. Nest is 22 inches wide and over 4 inches deep.

**Eggs:** 2–5 off-white-to-green eggs with brown spots

**Young:** Chicks are born with eyes closed and covered in down feathers, 20–23 days after laying. They leave the nest at 35 days and are independent at 7 weeks.

**Predators:** Eggs and chicks are the most vulnerable to raccoons, coyotes, and hawks. As adults, alligators, coyotes, and humans can be predators (due to illegal hunting).

**Migration:** Year-round resident of Florida. Though some will choose to migrate small distances for foraging areas.

Roseate spoonbills are large, pink wading birds. Both male and female adults have a featherless greenish-gray head. The neck, back, and breast are covered in white feathers. The rest of the body is covered in rose-colored feathers. During breeding season, they sport a deep hot-pink-colored shoulder patch. Juveniles are a paler pink and have a head covered with feathers.

### Did you know?

Rose-breasted grosbeaks are famous for their melodic songs. During the mating season, males may sing up to 689 songs in a day while advertising their breeding territories. Rose-breasted grosbeaks are very strong fliers; during migration, they are able to fly through the Gulf of Mexico without stopping, which is over 500 miles (805 km)!

Nest Type

Migrates

# Rose-breasted Grosbeak

*Pheucticus ludovicianus*

**Size:** 7–8½ inches long; wingspan of 11½–13 inches; weighs 1½–2 ounces

**Habitat:** Forests, forest edges, shrubby areas, swamps, and other wetlands

**Range:** Can be found throughout Florida and much of the northeastern United States. During the breeding season, it is a common bird in portions of the Midwest; during migration, it's common in the eastern US.

**Food:** Omnivores that eat mostly insects and other invertebrates (animals without bones) like spiders and snails. Seeds are also a big portion of their diet.

**Nesting:** Females lay 1 or 3 broods (groups) of 3–5 eggs a year. Both parents incubate and provide care to young.

**Nest:** Cup-shaped nest built out of twigs, weeds, and leaves

**Eggs:** Light greenish or bluish eggs that can be spotted with a brownish red

**Young:** Chicks are born with just a small number of feathers about 11 days after laying. They will leave the nest 9–12 days after hatching and will be completely independent around the 3-week mark.

**Predators:** Blue jays, hawks, grackles, squirrels

**Migration:** Migrates twice a year in the spring and fall, usually flying during the night hours

Males and females have different appearances, with the male having a white bill, black head, and a white belly with a rose-colored throat that extends down toward parts of the white breast. Females are not as colorful; they have a brown back and off-white-to-cream-colored belly with brown streaks.

**Did you know?**
The smallest bird that you can find in Florida is the ruby-throated hummingbird. During migration, male hummingbirds will utilize sapsucker (woodpecker) sap wells to get nutrients because of the lack of flowering plants in early spring. Hummingbirds can achieve 200 wing beats per second.

Nest Type

Migrates

# Ruby-throated Hummingbird

*Archilochus colubris*

**Size:** 3–3½ inches long; wingspan of 3⅛–4¼ inches; weighs ⅒ of an ounce

**Habitat:** Forested areas, orchards, gardens, and city parks

**Range:** They are breeding residents in much of the state of Florida. They are nonbreeding residents in the south-ernmost tip of Florida. They breed in the eastern United States, as well as eastern and central Canada.

**Food:** Drinks nectar from flowers and eats small insects and spiders

**Nesting:** March to August

**Nest:** A walnut-size nest is built in wooded areas, usually 10–20 feet off the ground; nest can be made of grasses, spiderwebs, and other vegetation. Nest is often cov-ered with lichen chips.

**Eggs:** 2 white eggs

**Young:** Young (chicks) will start flying around 20 days after hatching.

**Predators:** Cats, spiders, robber flies, praying mantises, dragon-flies, frogs, hawks, falcons, and kites (birds of prey)

**Migration:** Hummingbirds migrate to Mexico or Central America starting in August.

Ruby-throated hummingbirds are the only species of hum-mingbirds that nest in the eastern United States. Males have a magnificent ruby-colored throat made of iridescent (shimmering) feathers; males also have green iridescent feathers on their wings. Females are duller in comparison.

**Did you know?**
The sandhill crane is the most abundant crane species in the world. They are not afraid to defend themselves when threatened. They will use their feet and bill to ward off predators, often stabbing attackers with their bill. Sometimes sandhill cranes will travel 500 miles in one day to find food.

Nest Type

Migrates

# Sandhill Crane

*Grus canadensis*

**Size:** 3½–4 feet long; wingspan of 6–7 feet; weighs 7½–10 pounds

**Habitat:** Grasslands, savannas, and farm fields

**Range:** Breeding resident that can be found throughout Florida; found year-round in parts of Florida and Georgia. Can be found during migration in many states.

**Food:** Berries, insects, snails, amphibians, and small mammals as well as food crops like corn

**Nesting:** Nonmigratory populations will lay eggs from December to August, while populations that migrate will nest between April and May.

**Nest:** Both adults build the cup-shaped nest using vegetation from nearby areas.

**Eggs:** Up to 3 pale brownish-yellow eggs with brown spots

**Young:** Chicks are born with the ability to see and walk. Chicks become independent at around 9 months and will start breeding between 2 and 7 years.

**Predators:** Coyotes, raccoons, ravens, great horned owls, and humans

**Migration:** Sandhill cranes are found year-round in Florida.

The sandhill crane is a large bird with gray to brownish feathers with a white face and ruby-red crown. They are commonly seen in large groups in fields.

99

### Did you know?

White ibises will wash their food to eat. When they find an item that is very muddy, they will dunk it in the water before consuming it. White ibises are very social birds that live and nest in groups or colonies. Often other wading birds, like egrets, will follow behind them when they are foraging because they will stir up food that the egrets eat.

Nest Type

Migrates

100

# White Ibis

*Eudocimus albus*

**Size:** 22–24 inches tall; wingspan of 3 feet; weighs 3 pounds

**Habitat:** Marshes, swamps, mud flats, mangroves, coastal and estuarine areas, ponds, and flooded fields

**Range:** White ibises can be found along the Atlantic and Gulf Coasts of the US. They are found year-round in Florida.

**Food:** Carnivores that mostly feed on crawfish, crabs, insects, frogs, lizards, snails, and small fish

**Nesting:** Takes place in the spring when the female selects the site near water and usually in a shrub or tree branches. Nesting happens in colonies with other wading birds. Both parents provide care to chicks.

**Nest:** Both adults build a messy platform using vegetation. The nest is about 10 inches wide and 2–4 inches tall.

**Eggs:** 1–5 creamy to bluish-green eggs with brown spots

**Young:** Chicks hatch 3 weeks after laying, with eyes closed and covered in down feathers. They fledge around 28 days and become independent at around 7 weeks.

**Predators:** Crows, raccoons, alligators, snakes, black-crowned night-herons, opossums, owls, and humans

**Migration:** White ibises are found year-round in Florida.

White ibises are mostly white, except for the black tips of the wings. They have a long reddish-pink bill and legs. The skin around their blue eyes is also pink. Immatures are a marbled brown and white with a paler bill and legs.

## Did you know?

Turkeys sometimes fly at night, unlike most birds, and land in trees to roost. Turkeys have some interesting facial features; the red skin growth on a turkey's face above the beak is called a snood, while the growth under the beak is called a wattle. Wild turkeys can have more than 5,000 feathers.

Nest Type

# Wild Turkey

*Meleagris gallopavo*

**Size:** 3–4 feet long; wingspan of 5 feet; males weigh 16–25 pounds; females weigh 9–11 pounds

**Habitat:** Woodlands and grasslands

**Range:** Found throughout Florida. They also can be found in the eastern US and have been introduced in many western areas of the country.

**Food:** Grain, snakes, frogs, insects, acorns, berries, and ferns

**Nesting:** April to September

**Nest:** The nest is built on the ground using leaves as bedding, in brush or near the base of trees or fallen logs.

**Eggs:** 10–12 tan eggs with very small reddish-brown spots

**Young:** Poults (young) hatch about a month after eggs are laid; they will flock with the mother for a year. When young are still unable to fly, the mom will stay on the ground with her poults to provide protection and warmth. When poults grow up, they are known as a hen if they are female, or a gobbler or tom if they are male.

**Predators:** Humans, foxes, raccoons, owls, eagles, skunks, and fishers

**Migration:** Turkeys do not migrate.

A wild turkey is a large bird that is dark brown and black with some iridescent feathers. Males will fan out their tail to attract a mate. When threatened, they will also fan out their tail and rush the predator, sometimes kicking and puncturing prey with the spurs on their feet.

### Did you know?

Wood ducks will "mimic" a soccer player when a predator is near their young: they flop! Female wood ducks will fake a broken wing to lure predators away from their young. Wood duck hatchlings must jump from the nest after hatching to reach the water. They can jump 50 feet or more without hurting themselves.

Nest Type

Migrates

# Wood Duck

*Aix sponsa*

**Size:** 15–20 inches long; wingspan of 30 inches; weighs about 1 pound

**Habitat:** Swamps, woody ponds, and marshes

**Range:** They are year-long residents throughout Florida, except for the southernmost tip; they are also in the eastern US, southern Mexico, the Pacific Northwest, and on the West Coast.

**Food:** Fruits, nuts, and aquatic vegetation, especially duckweed, sedges, and grasses

**Nesting:** March to August

**Nest:** Wood ducks use hollow trees, abandoned woodpecker cavities, and human-made nesting boxes.

**Eggs:** 8–15 off-white eggs are laid once a year. Sometimes females will lay eggs in another female's nest; this process is called egg dumping.

**Young:** Eggs hatch about a month after being laid. Chicks will leave the nest after a day and fly within 8 weeks.

**Predators:** Raccoons, mink, fish, hawks, snapping turtles, owls, humans, and muskrats

**Migration:** They are year-round residents in much of Florida.

Wood duck males have a brightly colored crest (tuft of feathers) of iridescent (shimmering) green, red, and purple, with a mahogany (brown) upper breast area and tan bottom. Males also have red eyes. Females are brown to gray. Wood ducks have strong claws that enable them to climb up trees into cavities.

### Did you know?

Wood storks are the only species of storks that breed in the US. Wood storks will sometimes steal the nest of another wood stork, throwing the eggs and young out of the nest. While their legs are actually black, oftentimes they look white because they will use the restroom on themselves as a way to keep cool. The white color comes from a chemical called uric acid, which turns into a white paste mixed in with their waste.

Nest Type

Migrates

# Wood Stork

*Mycteria americana*

**Size:** 33½–45½ inches tall; wingspan of 60–65 inches; weighs about 4–6 pounds

**Habitat:** Freshwater marshes, mangroves, flooded fields, ponds, lakes, lagoons, streams, swamps, and rivers

**Range:** The United States has breeding populations in Florida, Georgia, and North and South Carolina. In Florida, they are found throughout the state.

**Food:** Mostly carnivores; fish, rodents, crawfish, turtles, crabs, aquatic insects, snakes, baby alligators, and frogs. They sometimes eat plant material.

**Nesting:** November to August, they nest colonially in trees.

**Nest:** Platform nest is built by both male and female using twigs and sticks. The inside is lined with leaves and twigs. Nests are usually at least 10 feet above water.

**Eggs:** Female lays one clutch of 3–5 creamy-white eggs. Eggs are incubated for 27–32 days by both male and female.

**Young:** Eggs hatch about a month after being laid. Chicks will leave the nest after a day and fly within 8 weeks. Fledging takes place 2 months after hatching. They reach reproductive age around 4 years.

**Predators:** Raccoons, skunks, fish, snapping turtles, alligators, humans, snakes, and other wood storks

**Migration:** Mostly non-migrating, but juvenile birds have been observed moving north of nesting areas.

The wood stork is a large white bird with a bare head and neck of slate gray. Wings and tail are iridescent black to green. Feet, bill, and legs are black, and the toes are pink during breeding season. Immatures have a feather head and yellow-gray bill.

**Did you know?**

Alligator snapping turtles are the largest freshwater turtle species not only in Florida, but also in North America! They can weigh up to 200 pounds. Being that big, it has a bite force of 1,000 pounds. That's not the only amazing thing about their mouth; an alligator snapping turtle has a built-in "lure" (or skin protrusion) on its tongue that acts like bait to attract prey.

Most Active      Hibernates

108

# Alligator Snapping Turtle

*Macrochelys temminckii*

**Size:** Male: 31 inches long; weighs 150–200 pounds.
Female: 20–22 inches long; weighs 60–63 pounds

**Habitat:** Rivers, streams, lakes, bayous, and swamps

**Range:** Alligator snapping turtles are endemic, or only found in the US. They are found throughout the Florida Panhandle, with their range extending in areas of the northern peninsula.

**Food:** Mostly carnivorous; feeds on aquatic animals like fish, crawdads (crawfish), clams, mussels, and some plant materials, as well as birds and snakes

**Mating:** April to June and have to travel to find mates

**Nest:** Females will travel away from water sources on land and dig nest in sand or dirt.

**Eggs:** 1 clutch per year of around 10–60 spherical, whitish eggs with a leathery shell

**Young:** Eggs will hatch around 100 days after laying. Nest temperature determines sex at hatching: male turtles develop in cooler nest temperatures and females develop at warmer nest temperatures. They are fully independent at hatching, do not receive any care from parents, and reach sexual maturity around ages 11–16.

**Predators:** Raccoons, birds, otters, and fish will prey on eggs and juveniles. Adults are hunted by humans.

They have a spiked, dark-brown carapace. Alligator snapping turtles have 3 rows of raised scutes that resemble spikes on their carapace (back shell) that are brown to greenish gray. The plastron (bottom shell) is lighter than the carapace. They have a large triangular or spade-shaped head with a hooked beak. **109**

### Did you know?

The male alligator does not have vocal cords. The growling or roaring sound that males make in order to attract females comes from the alligator filling its lungs with air and exhaling. Alligators sometimes trick birds into landing or flying close to them by placing sticks and vegetation on their head; birds looking for nesting material will fly and try to retrieve the sticks and be met by the gator's mouth.

Most Active

110

# American Alligator

*Alligator mississippiensis*

**Size:** 8–16 feet long; weighs up to 1,000 pounds

**Habitat:** Freshwater ponds, coastal areas, rivers, swamps, and brackish water (mix of fresh and saltwater)

**Range:** They are native to the southeastern United States from Florida to North Carolina and as far west as Texas. In Florida, they can be found statewide.

**Food:** Opportunistic carnivores that feed on snakes, fish, birds, mammals, insects, and sometimes even fruit

**Mating:** Starts in spring and goes until May or early June. Mating takes place at night. Males have multiple mates.

**Nest:** Nests are made of plant material and can be 3 feet tall by 7 feet wide. Eggs are covered with vegetation.

**Eggs:** 35–50 white eggs

**Young:** Eggs hatch about 2 months after laying. Hatchling sex is temperature dependent; nest temperatures below 88 degrees or above 90½ degrees are usually female, and temperatures of 89½ to around 90½ degrees are usually male. They reach independence at 1 year and reproductive age at around 10 years. Hatchlings form pods or groups and alert others to nearby danger by making clicking noises.

**Predators:** Humans; as juveniles: birds, snakes, bobcats, raccoons, otters, large fish, and older alligators

The American alligator is a thick-bodied reptile with short legs. It has a wide U-shaped snout. The body has thick skin that comes in colors of black to brownish gray; the tail is thick and muscular; the underside is white. Hatchlings are striped for the first several months. If the water freezes, alligators will bury themselves in mud and stick their snouts out for several days.

**Did you know?**

Cottonmouths are toxic but have a similar pattern to many different species of nonvenomous water snakes. One distinct feature that gives them away is the white lining of the mouth (hence the name cottonmouth), as well as the cream, white, or light-tan colors of the external (outside) portion of the mouth.

Most Active    Hibernates

# Cottonmouth (Water Moccasin)

*Agkistrodon piscivorus*

**Size:** 2–4 feet long; weighs 2–4 pounds

**Habitat:** Forest, prairies, creeks, streams, marshes, swamps, coastal areas, and the shores of ponds and lakes

**Range:** Can be found in the eastern US. In Florida, they are found statewide.

**Food:** Birds, small turtles, fish, frogs, small mammals, snakes, lizards, and small alligators

**Mating:** April–May; males perform mating dances and fight over females.

**Nest:** No nest; they will use natural cavities in the ground or abandoned burrows of small mammals.

**Eggs:** No eggs are laid.

**Young:** They are ovoviviparous, meaning the eggs develop in the body and then the mother gives live birth. Usually 5–9 live young are born, but as many as 16 can be born at one time. Snakelets are born 6 months after mating. At birth they are independent and receive no parental care.

**Predators:** Domestic cats, hawks, egrets, raccoons, eagles, large fish like longnose gars and largemouth bass, herons, and snapping turtles

Cottonmouth bodies come in various shades of dark colors from brown to black. The head is brown to tan with shades of yellowish browns. The bottom of the head is various shades of lighter hues of white, tan, brown, and cream colors with distinct facial markings. Cottonmouths have a series of 10 or more bands across their back. Their eyes are like those of cats, with vertical pupils.

**Did you know?**
The eastern coral snake is venomous, even though it does not have an arrow-shaped head. This proves that what's true for some venomous snakes is not true for all venomous snakes. Western coral snakes are the only snakes in the eastern part of the US that have fangs fixed in the front of their mouth.

Most Active

Hibernates

# Eastern Coral Snake

*Micrurus fulvius*

**Size:** 18–30 inches long (rarely over 17 inches); weight ranges widely

**Habitat:** Grasslands, suburban areas, flatwoods and scrub areas, woodlands, forests, wetlands and the borders of swamps, and coastal plain areas like sandhills

**Range:** Eastern coral snakes can be found from the southeastern parts of North Carolina through Florida and the southern parts of Georgia, as well as Alabama and Mississippi into the southeastern areas of Louisiana. They are widespread throughout the state of Florida.

**Food:** Frogs, snakes, lizards, insects, and sometimes mammals

**Mating:** Late spring to early fall

**Nest:** No nest; they will use natural cavities in the ground or abandoned burrows of small mammals. The eggs are often laid underground or in leaf litter.

**Eggs:** 4–12 white, leathery eggs that are elongated

**Young:** Snakelets hatch around 2 months after laying. They are around 7–9 inches at hatching. No parental care is given. Females become mature around 21 months and males become mature around 11–21 months.

**Predators:** Snakes, raptors like American kestrels and hawks, bullfrogs, loggerhead shrikes, and cats. Eggs and juveniles are vulnerable to red ants.

Eastern coral snakes have a striped body with a pattern of red, black, and yellow bands or rings. The red and yellow touch, followed by the black. The nose is black with the rest of the head being yellow. The red stripes have black specks within them. Juveniles have a similar pattern as the adults but brighter in color. The pattern darkens as the snake ages.

### Did you know?

Eastern garter snakes are highly social and will form groups with other snakes and often other species to overwinter together in a burrow or hole. When threatened by a predator or handled, they will sometimes musk or emit a foul-smelling, oily substance from their cloaca (butt).

Most Active    Hibernates

116

# Eastern Garter Snake

*Thamnophis sirtalis*

**Size:** 14–36 inches long (rarely over 17 inches); weighs 5–5½ ounces

**Habitat:** Forests and forest edges, grasslands, and suburban areas

**Range:** They are found throughout Florida, except for a small area on the Gulf Coast area of the peninsula and can be found in the eastern US from Minnesota, southward to eastern Texas, and then east towards the Atlantic Coast.

**Food:** Frogs, snails, toads, salamanders, insects, fish, and worms

**Mating:** April or May

**Nest:** No nest; they will use natural cavities in the ground or abandoned burrows of small mammals.

**Eggs:** No eggs are laid. Eastern Garter Snakes are born live in a litter of between 8 and 20 snakes.

**Young:** Snakelets are 4½–9 inches long at birth; no parental care is given.

**Predators:** Crows, ravens, hawks, owls, raccoons, foxes, and squirrels

Eastern garter snakes are black with three yellow stripes running down their body on the back and sides. They withstand winter by gathering in groups inside the burrows of rodents or under human-made structures, and they enter brumation, or a state of slowed body activity.

**Did you know?**
The eastern indigo snake is the longest native snake species that is found in North America. Eastern indigo snakes get their name from the iridescence that they have on their scales. In the right light, the color looks deep blue or purplish.

Most Active     Hibernates

# Eastern Indigo Snake

*Drymarchon couperi*

**Size:** 5–7 feet long; weighs 6–10 pounds

**Habitat:** Sandhill habitats, shady creek bottoms, flatwoods, stream bottoms, cane fields, forests, wetlands, shrublands, prairies, pine forests, coastal dunes, and areas with gopher tortoises

**Range:** Eastern indigo snakes range from extreme southwestern South Carolina south through Florida and west to southern Alabama and southeastern Mississippi. In Florida, they are found throughout the state.

**Food:** Carnivore that feeds on turtles, toads, lizards, eggs, frogs, mammals, snakes, and birds

**Mating:** November–April

**Nest:** Abandoned burrows or fallen logs

**Eggs:** 6–12 eggs per clutch

**Young:** Snakelets hatch after around 3 months. They are between 16 inches and 2 feet long and are completely independent when hatched. They reach maturity around year 3 or 4.

**Predators:** Alligators, snakes, domesticated dogs and cats, red-tailed hawks, humans

The eastern indigo snake has a brick-red-to-orange throat and cheeks; their underside is a charcoal-blackish gray. Immature indigos are a glossy black with white-and-hazy-blue bands down their body.

**Did you know?**

Kingsnakes get their name because they eat a variety of different snake species, many of which are venomous. It's a good thing kingsnakes have a resistance to venom. Eastern kingsnakes will mimic rattlesnakes when disturbed, vibrating their tails.

Most Active

Hibernates

# Eastern Kingsnake

*Lampropeltis getula*

**Size:** 36–48 inches long; weighs 4–5 pounds

**Habitat:** Hardwood forests, swamps, pine forest, fields, freshwater marshes, and city areas

**Range:** Southern New Jersey to Northern Florida, west to the Appalachians. In Florida they are found in the Panhandle and the northern portion of the peninsula.

**Food:** Rodents, birds, snakes, lizards, and turtle eggs

**Mating:** March–May

**Nest:** Nests are usually in abandoned burrows, under a log, or made in moist soil.

**Eggs:** 4–20 white eggs

**Young:** Hatchlings emerge 60 days after eggs are laid; the young are brightly colored and weighing around 9–14 grams and approximately 5–8 inches long. Females become reproductively mature around 2–3 years and males around 1–2 years.

**Predators:** Raccoons, snakes, hawks, alligators, skunks, and opossums

The eastern kingsnake is a thick black snake with small eyes. Scales are smooth. It has white-to-yellow bands across the back. Snakes from mountainous areas usually have thinner bands or are almost completely black, and snakes from the coastal plain have wider bands.

### Did you know?

The eastern tiger salamander can grow up to 13 inches long and live over 20 years! Eastern tiger salamanders migrate to their birthplace in order to breed, sometimes over a mile or more. Eastern tiger salamanders have a hidden weapon! They produce a poisonous toxin that is secreted or released from two glands in their tail. This toxin makes them taste bad to predators and allows them to escape.

Most Active     Hibernates

# Eastern Tiger Salamander

*Ambystoma tigrinum*

**Size:** 7–13 inches long; weighs 4½ ounces

**Habitat:** Woodlands, marshes, and meadows; they spend most of their time underground in burrows.

**Range:** They are found in many states along the Atlantic Coast. In Florida, they can be found in the Panhandle and northwestern parts of the peninsula. They can also be found westward to Arizona and as far north as Canada.

**Food:** Carnivores (eat meat); insects, frogs, worms, and snails

**Mating:** Tiger salamanders leave their burrows to find standing bodies of fresh water. They breed in late winter and early spring after the ground has thawed.

**Nest:** No nest, but eggs are joined together into one group in a jelly-like sack called an egg mass. An egg mass is attached to grass, leaves, and other plant material at the bottom of a pond.

**Eggs:** There are 20–100 eggs or more in an egg mass.

**Young:** Eggs hatch after 2 weeks, and the young are fully aquatic with external gills. Limbs develop shortly after hatching; within 3 months, the young are fully grown but will hang around in a vernal pool. Individuals living in permanent ponds can take up to 6 months to fully develop.

**Predators:** Young are preyed upon by diving beetles, fish, turtles, and herons. Adults are preyed upon by snakes, owls, and badgers.

Eastern tiger salamanders have thick black, brown, or grayish bodies with uneven spots of yellow, tan, brown, or green along the head and body. The underside is usually a variation of yellow. Males are usually larger and thicker than females.

**Did you know?**
Gopher tortoises are keystone species, meaning that other animals depend on them for their survival. Over 350 species of animals depend on or benefit from the burrows that gopher tortoises make. These burrows are on average 15 feet long and over 6 feet deep. Some tortoises make burrows that are over 30 feet long and 10 feet deep. The gopher tortoise is the only native species of tortoises that can be found east of the Mississippi River.

Most Active    Hibernates

# Gopher Tortoise

*Gopherus polyphemus*

**Size:** 9–15 inches long; weighs 10–13 pounds

**Habitat:** Longleaf pine sandhills, scrub, pine flatwoods, coastal grasslands, dunes, and prairies

**Range:** Gopher tortoises can be found in the coastal plain area of the United States from the most southern areas of South Carolina, south into Florida, and westward to eastern Louisiana. In Florida, they can be found throughout much of the state, except for a few isolated areas on the Georgia border, in the south-central area, and on the southern tip of the state.

**Food:** Herbivores (plant eaters) that feed on grasses, fruits, and flowers. Sometimes they will eat carrion (dead things).

**Mating:** March–October

**Nest:** Usually built in bare, sunny areas; the mounded area in front is called a burrow apron.

**Eggs:** 5–9 white, sphere-shaped, Ping-Pong-ball-size eggs

**Young:** Hatchlings emerge about 2 inches long 90–110 days after laying. They are independent at the time of hatching. Males reach adulthood in around 9–12 years and females at around 10–21 years.

**Predators:** Eagles, raccoons, bears, hawks, foxes, coyotes, bobcats, armadillos, fire ants, skunks, and dogs

Gopher tortoises have a smushed dome-shaped carapace that is somewhat flattened and comes in shades of brown and gray. The skin is scaly and can be shades of gray to tan and brown. They have forelimbs that are flat and aid in digging. Juveniles have yellow-hued skin and scutes (hard plates on the shell) that are yellow in the center and get darker with age.

### Did you know?

The green anole is the only species of anole that is native to the United States. The male does pushups to attract a mate and defend its territory. They will extend the dewlap (a skin fold under the chin) and bob their head up and down in the presence of a rival male. Green anoles can change colors! Although not as elaborate as chameleons, they can change to various shades of green and brown.

Most Active

# Green Anole

*Anolis carolinensis*

**Size:** 5–8 inches long; weighs 1-6 grams, or about as much as a penny or two

**Habitat:** Moist forests, coastal areas, shrublands, urban areas, swamps, and farmlands

**Range:** Anoles are found throughout the southeastern US. In Florida they are found statewide.

**Food:** Carnivore that feeds on insects and other soft-bodied animals like spiders, flies, crickets, and grasshoppers.

**Mating:** April–September, males will patrol a territory and defend it from other males. Males attract females by extending their dewlap (pink-colored skin under chin) and bobbing up and down.

**Nest:** Shallow depression in soft soil, leaf litter, compost, rotting wood, or even a hole in a nearby tree

**Eggs:** 1–10 soft-shelled eggs are laid 2 to 4 weeks after mating.

**Young:** Hatching takes place 30–45 days after laying. Anoles are 2–2½ inches at hatching and are fully independent.

**Predators:** Lizards, birds, cats, dogs, frogs, and snakes

Green anoles come in many shades of greens and browns. What color you see depends on their surroundings and the condition that they are in. Males have a bright-red-to-ruby-pink skinfold or dewlap that extends under the chin. This dewlap serves a dual purpose of finding mates and deterring rival males from entering its territory. The female dewlap is much smaller and comes in shades of pink to almost white. Females have a white stripe that runs along their back.

**Did you know?**
Green tree frogs are sometimes called "rain frogs" because they have been observed singing louder during rain events. The green tree frog's mating call can be heard over 300 yards away and can be repeated over 70 times per minute.

Most Active

# Green Tree Frog

*Dryophytes cinereus*

**Size:** 1–2½ inches long; weight: limited information

**Habitat:** Prairies, marshes, lake and pond edges, swamps, urban and suburban areas

**Range:** Can be found throughout the central United States as far west as Texas and eastward into the Atlantic states of the eastern US. They are found throughout Florida.

**Food:** Carnivore that eats beetles and their larvae, flies, crickets, and caterpillars

**Mating:** March to October

**Nest:** No nest is built; will lay multiple clusters of eggs in one night in water.

**Eggs:** A few hundred to 3,000 eggs per cluster

**Young:** About a week after fertilization, eggs hatch. Within 8–10 weeks, tadpoles will grow legs. When the legs become functional, they will leave the water for land.

**Predators:** Snakes, lizards, herons, and fish

Green tree frogs are small- to medium-size frogs. They have a green upper body with patches of white and off-white on their skin. Underneath, the body is a yellow to white color. They have a cream-colored line that runs from the jaw to the end of the body. Males have wrinkled skin in the throat area for their vocal sac. Both sexes have toe pads. Males are smaller than females.

**Did you know?**
Leatherback sea turtles are the largest turtles in the world. They are the only sea turtle species that does not have a hard shell or scales; instead, they have a carapace that is made of tough skin that covers its bony plates. This is where they get their name "leatherback." Leatherbacks are extreme divers and can dive over 3,500 feet deep and can swim over 10,000 miles in a year while migrating to and from nesting and feeding areas.

Most Active       Migrates

# Leatherback Sea Turtle

*Dermochelys coriacea*

**Size:** 5–6½ feet long; weighs 750–2,000 pounds

**Habitat:** Open ocean and coastal waters

**Range:** Leatherbacks can be found in the surrounding oceans of the US. Florida, the Virgin Islands, and Puerto Rico receive the most nesting activity.

**Food:** Mostly carnivorous; jellyfish, crustaceans, and some seaweed

**Mating:** Mating and nesting occur in March through July.

**Nest:** Females nest at night by digging a massive pit to deposit their eggs into. They can nest as many as 4 times a season with 8–12 days in between.

**Eggs:** 100 eggs are laid. Eggs incubate for about 2 months. Only 80–85% of the eggs are fertilized.

**Young:** Like other reptiles, the temperature of the nest determines the sex of the sea turtle hatchlings. Once they leave the nest, they enter the water and fend for themselves until they reach reproductive age at around 7–15 years.

**Predators:** Nests and hatchlings are preyed upon by birds, raccoons, domestic pets, and crabs. Nesting adults fall victim to jaguars. While out at sea, adults are preyed on by large sharks and killer whales. Humans harm leatherbacks by littering and sometimes harvesting eggs.

The leatherback is a large turtle, with a scaled carapace that is covered by skin. The carapace is more triangular or shield shaped than circular like those of hard-shelled sea turtle species. The limbs are black and the plastron shell on the bottom is white. The body is adorned with white spots around the body. Young are black with white lines running down their back.

## Did you know?

Loggerhead turtles get their odd name because sailors originally mistook them for logs or tree trunks. Unlike other sea turtles, green sea turtles are mostly herbivores (plant eaters). They eat algae and other plants, which gives their fat and muscles a greenish tint, leading to their name!

Most Active

# Loggerhead Sea Turtle (LST)/ Green Sea Turtle (GST)

*Caretta caretta*

**Size:** LST: 2½–3½ feet long; weighs 200–375 pounds. GST: 3–4½ feet long; weighs 250–500 pounds

**Habitat:** Coastal areas and open ocean

**Range:** LST: They can be seen on the Florida coast, especially in summer. GST: Found around the world where the water is warm enough.

**Food:** LST: Crabs, jellyfish, conches, fish. GST: Seagrass and algae

**Mating:** (LST) May–August and (GST) June–September. Mating takes place every 2–4 years.

**Nest:** LST: A cavity around 18 inches deep. GST: A cavity about 30 inches deep. Both species nest above the surf line (where waves crash) on beaches. Females can lay multiple batches of eggs a season and usually will lay a new nest after about 14 days or so.

**Eggs:** LST: 100-130 eggs; GST: 100-130 eggs. Ping-Pong-ball size

**Young:** After 2 months of incubating, hatchlings emerge and immediately travel toward the ocean.

**Predators:** Feral hogs, sharks, raccoons, dogs, humans, crows, birds, fish, ants, crabs, cats, coyotes, foxes, bears, and skunks

Loggerheads have a distinctive large head and heart-shaped carapace (shell) that ranges from brown to red. The underside is paler and yellow to off-white. Green sea turtles are the second-largest sea turtle (the leatherback is bigger). Their shell is dark brown to olive colored with a yellow-to-pale plastron (underside).

### Did you know?

When threatened, a rattlesnake shakes its rattle to warn would-be predators. These snakes are all venomous (their bites inject venom, a toxin), so do not go near one or try to pick one up! Instead, leave it alone, so it can help people by munching on rodents and other pests! Rattlesnakes are "pit vipers," snakes that have a special body part that helps them "see" heat.

Most Active   Hibernates

# Rattlesnakes

Eastern Diamondback Rattlesnake (EDR) (*Crotalus adamanteus*), Timber Rattlesnake (TR) (*Crotalus horridus*), Pygmy Rattlesnake (PR) (*Sistrurus miliarius*)

**Size:** EDR: 33–72 inches long; weighs 10 pounds. TR: 36–40 inches long; weighs 1–2 pounds. PR: 14–22 inches long; weighs 5½ ounces

**Habitat:** EDR: Elevated areas near floodplains and swamps, forests, dunes; TR: Lowland forests near water; PR: Scrublands, coastal areas, forests, swamps

**Range:** EDR: Only found in the southeastern US. In Florida they are found throughout. TR: Found in the northern areas of Florida. Their range extends as far north as New Hampshire, and as far west as central Texas. PR: The eastern US. Found throughout Florida

**Food:** EDR: Small mammals, birds. TR: Small mammals, birds, other snakes, lizards, and frogs. PR: Insects, small mammals, frogs, and lizards

**Mating:** September–January; display a courtship "dance."

**Nest:** The mother gives birth in a burrow or hollow log.

**Eggs:** They are ovoviviparous, so snakes are born live.

**Young:** EDR: 6–21 snakelets; around 15 inches. TR: 12 or more young; 10–18 inches. PR: 1–12 young

**Predators:** Coyotes, humans, bobcats, skunks, foxes, hawks, and owls; kingsnakes, indigo snakes, and cottonmouths

Eastern diamondback: Brown, yellow, or tan, with black, gray, or brownish diamond. Timber: Gray, brown, or pink, with brown or orange stripes. Pygmy: Gray to black with hints of orange, and brown lines down the back. All have catlike pupils.

### Did you know?

The snapping turtle's sex is determined by the temperature of the nest! Nest temperatures that are 67–68 degrees produce females, temperatures in the range between 70 and 72 degrees produce both males and females, and nests that are 73–75 degrees will usually produce all males.

Most Active

# Snapping Turtle, Common

*Chelydra serpentina*

**Size:** 8–16 inches long; weighs 10–35 pounds

**Habitat:** Rivers, marshes, and lakes; can be found in areas that have brackish water (freshwater and saltwater mixture)

**Range:** They are found throughout Florida; also found in the eastern US and southern Canada.

**Food:** These omnivores (eat both plants and animals) eat frogs, reptiles, snakes, birds, small mammals, and plants.

**Mating:** April to November are the breeding months; lays eggs during June and July

**Nest:** Females dig a hole in sandy soil and lay the eggs into it.

**Eggs:** 25–42 eggs, sometimes as many as 80 or more

**Young:** Like sea turtles, snapping turtles have temperature-dependent sex determination (TSD), meaning the temperature of the nest determines the sex of the young. Hatchlings leave the nest between August and October. In the North, turtles mature at around 15–20 years, while southern turtles mature around 12 years old.

**Predators:** Raccoons, skunks, crows, dogs, and humans

The snapping turtle's carapace (top shell) is dark green to brown and usually covered in algae or moss. The plastron (or bottom of the shell) is smaller than the carapace. They are crepuscular animals that are mostly active during the dawn and dusk hours. Young turtles will actively look for food. As adults, they rely heavily on ambushing to hunt; they bury themselves in the sand with just the tip of their nose and eyes showing.

# Glossary

**Adaptation**—An animal's physical (outward) or behavioral (inward) adjustment to changes in the environment.

**Amphibian**—A small animal with a backbone, has moist skin, and lacks scales. Most amphibians start out as an egg, live at least part of their life in water, and finish life as a land dweller.

**Biome**—A part or region of Earth that has a particular type of climate and animals and plants that adapted to live in the area.

**Bird**—A group of animals that all have two legs and feet, a beak, feathers, and wings; while not all birds fly, all birds lay eggs.

**Brood**—A group of young birds that hatch at the same time and with the same mother.

**Carnivore**—An animal that primarily eats other animals.

**Clutch**—The number of eggs an animal lays during one nesting period; an animal can lay more than one clutch each season.

**Crepuscular**—The hours before sunset or just after sunrise; some animals have adapted to be most active during these low-light times.

**Diurnal**—During the day; many animals are most active during the daytime.

**Ecosystem**—A group of animals and plants that interact with each other and the physical area that they live in.

**Evolution**—A process of change in a species or a group of animals that are all the same kind; evolution happens over several generations or in a group of animals living around the same time; evolution happens through adaptation, or physical and biological changes to better fit the environment over time.

**Fledgling**—A baby bird that has developed flight feathers and has left the nest.

**Gestation**—The length of time a developing animal is carried in its mother's womb.

**Herbivore**—An animal that primarily eats plants.

**Hibernate**—A survival strategy or process where animals "slow down" and go into a long period of reduced activity to survive winter or seasonal changes; during hibernation, activities like feeding, breathing, and converting food to energy all stop.

**Insectivore**—An animal whose diet consists of insects.

**Incubate**—When a bird warms eggs by sitting on them.

**Invasive**—A nonnative animal that outcompetes native animals in a particular area, harming the environment.

**Mammal**—An air-breathing, warm-blooded, fur- or hair-covered animal with a backbone. All mammals produce milk and usually give birth to live young.

**Migration**—When animals move from one area to another. Migration usually occurs seasonally, but it can also happen due to biological processes, such as breeding.

**Molt**—When animals shed or drop their skin, feathers, or shell.

**Nocturnal**—At night; many animals are most active at night.

**Nonnative**—An organism introduced (by humans) into a new area.

**Omnivore**—An animal that eats both plants and other animals.

**Piscivore**—An animal that eats mainly fish

**Predator**—An animal that hunts (and eats) other animals.

**Raptor**—A group of birds that all have a curved beak and sharp talons, which hunt or feed on other animals. Also known as a bird of prey.

**Reptile**—An egg-laying, air-breathing, cold-blooded animal that has a backbone and skin made of scales, which crawls on its belly or uses stubby legs to get around.

**Scat**—The waste product that animals release from their bodies; another word for it is poop or droppings.

**Talon**—The claw on the feet see on raptors and birds of prey.

**Torpor**—A form of hibernation in which an animal slows down its breathing, and heart rate; torpor ranges from a few hours at a time to a whole day; torpor does not involve a deep sleep.

# Checklist

## Mammals

- ☐ American Beaver
- ☐ Black Bear
- ☐ Bobcat
- ☐ Coyote
- ☐ Eastern Cottontail
- ☐ Eastern Fox Squirrel
- ☐ Eastern Mole
- ☐ Florida Panther
- ☐ Gray Fox
- ☐ Key Deer
- ☐ Manatee (West Indian Manatee)
- ☐ Mexican Free-tailed Bat
- ☐ Northern Raccoon
- ☐ Northern River Otter
- ☐ Red Fox
- ☐ Southeastern Beach Mouse
- ☐ Southern Flying Squirrel
- ☐ Spotted Skunk
- ☐ Striped Skunk
- ☐ Tricolored Bat
- ☐ Virginia Opossum
- ☐ White-tailed Deer

## Birds

- ☐ American Goldfinch
- ☐ Anhinga
- ☐ Bald Eagle
- ☐ Barred Owl
- ☐ Belted Kingfisher
- ☐ Black Vulture/ Turkey Vulture
- ☐ Blue Grosbeak
- ☐ Brown Pelican
- ☐ Burrowing Owl
- ☐ Great Blue Heron
- ☐ Magnificent Frigatebird
- ☐ Mallard
- ☐ Mississippi Kite/ Swallow-tailed Kite
- ☐ Northern Cardinal
- ☐ Osprey
- ☐ Painted Bunting
- ☐ Peregrine Falcon
- ☐ Red-tailed Hawk/ Red-shouldered Hawk
- ☐ Roseate Spoonbill
- ☐ Rose-breasted Grosbeak

- ☐ Ruby-throated Hummingbird
- ☐ Sandhill Crane
- ☐ White Ibis
- ☐ Wild Turkey
- ☐ Wood Duck
- ☐ Wood Stork

**Reptiles and Amphibians**

- ☐ Alligator Snapping Turtle
- ☐ American Alligator
- ☐ Cottonmouth (Water Moccasin)
- ☐ Eastern Coral Snake
- ☐ Eastern Garter Snake
- ☐ Eastern Indigo Snake
- ☐ Eastern Kingsnake
- ☐ Eastern Tiger Salamander
- ☐ Gopher Tortoise
- ☐ Green Anole
- ☐ Green Tree Frog
- ☐ Leatherback Sea Turtle
- ☐ Loggerhead Sea Turtle/ Green Sea Turtle
- ☐ Rattlesnakes
- ☐ Snapping Turtle, Common

# The Art of Conservation®

Featuring two signature programs, The Songbird Art Contest™ and The Fish Art Contest®, the Art of Conservation programs celebrate the arts as a cornerstone to conservation. To enter, youth artists create an original hand-drawn illustration and written essay, story, or poem synthesizing what they have learned. The contests are FREE to enter and open to students in K-12. For program updates, rules, guidelines, and entry forms, visit: www.TheArtofConservation.org

**The Fish Art Contest®** introduces youth to the wonders of fish, the joy of fishing, and the importance of aquatic conservation. The Fish Art Contest uses art, science, and creative writing to foster connections to the outdoors and inspire the next generation of stewards. Participants are encouraged to use the Fish On! lesson plan, then submit an original, handmade piece of artwork to compete for prizes and international recognition.

**The Songbird Art Contest®** explores the wonders and species diversity of North American songbirds. Raising awareness and educating the public on bird conservation, the Songbird program builds stewardship, encourages outdoors participation, and promotes the discovery of nature.

# Photo Credits

## About the Author

**Alex Troutman** is a wildlife biologist, birder, nature enthusiast, and science communicator from Austell, Georgia. He has a passion for sharing the wonders of nature and introducing the younger generation to the outdoors. He holds both a bachelor's degree and a master's degree in biology from Georgia Southern University (the Real GSU), with a focus in conservation. Because he knows what it feels like to not see individuals who look like you, or come from a similar background, doing  the things you enjoy or working in the career that you aspire to be in, Alex makes a point not only to be that representation for the younger generation, but also to make sure that kids have exposure to the careers they are interested in and the diverse scientists working in those careers.

Alex is the co-organizer of several Black in X weeks, including Black Birders Week, Black Mammologists Week, and Black in Marine Science Week. This movement encourages diversity in nature, the celebration of Black individual scientists, awareness of Black nature enthusiasts, and diversity in STEAM fields.